Beneath A Surface

Brad Sams

Beneath A Surface

Brad Sams

This book was made possible by the unconditional love from wife, daughter, and the help of nearly two-dozen interviewees who asked to remain anonymous.

And to Paul Thurrott, who helped piece this book together and edited the content.

Thank You.

Contents

Chapter 1 - Early Ambitions

A decade before Apple released the iPad, Microsoft had its own Tablet PC platform. These devices were made by a variety of PC maker—or Original Equipment Manufacturer (OEM)—partners and they conformed to a specification outlined by Microsoft that included pen input, touchscreens, and several other requirements. Microsoft saw that the future of computing required more natural interfaces than the keyboard and mouse, and it spent the next decade chasing this dream.

When Apple finally introduced the iPad in 2010, Steve Jobs argued that the "Post-PC" era had begun. If true, the primary computing device was no longer a laptop or desktop computer (either Mac or Windows) but was instead a tablet. On stage and during interviews, Jobs' had a charismatic approach that is studied to this day because he had a way of telling people what they wanted and of convincing them at the same time that he was right, even when he was sometimes wrong. But when it came to tablets, Apple was taking the vision Microsoft saw many years prior and was grabbing headlines for its latest "genius" invention.

This narrative ran wild in the press with many publications announcing that Jobs had spoken the gospel and that the computing industry was about to be overhauled by new tablet experiences. Granted, Apple was on top of the world at this time, with the iPod having saved the company from bankruptcy (after Microsoft loaned it some cash) and the iPhone quickly toppling mobile industry incumbents like Blackberry, Nokia, and Microsoft. If Steve Jobs said it, it must be true.

The Post-PC era that Jobs' is frequently cited with creating was actually coined back in 1999 by an MIT scientist by the name of David D. Clark. This phrase was used to describe devices like tablets, digital televisions, streaming radio, and a "digital wave" that connected nearly everything to the Internet.

In an interview in 2012, Clark said that he used the term initially to "tweak his friends at Intel," which has a bit of humor hidden in the details. At that time, Clark was using this term to show how Intel, which had "won" the PC wars by being the company whose chips were in most of the PC hardware that was sold, would eventually lose control of this segment.

Seven years after this interview, Clark's tweaking of Intel with the post-PC era terminology is coming true as devices built using Advanced RISC Machines (ARM) processors are now found in everything from smartphones, laptops, tablets, and televisions.

But at that time, all Windows PCs were using Intel-type (x86 or x64) platforms, which means Microsoft found itself in a tough position. Would it risk creating Windows for the ARM platform and upset its longtime partner Intel? Or would it stay the course and hope that the overall market would return to an x86 world?

The answer was obvious for Microsoft. The company knew that the market would shift to a touch-based world, so its operating system, Windows, must adapt as well. But the clock was ticking. At first, the iPad was selling better than expected and Apple's hardware was quickly taking over the hearts and minds of consumers, and Microsoft needed to do something. But the company didn't have an operating system for consumers that ran on the ARM platform, and big decisions needed to be made to make sure that Microsoft had a future in this new world of more personal computing.

And it wasn't just Apple that was coming after Microsoft. Android, while still in its infancy on tablets, was gaining momentum as well. With Google acquiring the platform in 2005, the smartphone world was being consumed by the "free" operating system from Google while Microsoft was still charging its partners to license its own platforms, a model which eventually proved to be outdated.

As Android smartphones became the new popular choice and Apple's iPhone was selling well as a premium option, Microsoft found its position in the smartphone segment evaporating. And with many expecting that tablets would be the next giant wave of computing that would replace the PC, Microsoft had to do something, even if it meant upsetting its longtime partner Intel. Not to mention its many PC maker partners.

In January 2011, Microsoft was ready to show the world that it was going to move forward and that Windows could compete in the Post-PC era. At that month's Consumer Electronics Show (CES), Microsoft announced support for new System on a Chip (SoC) hardware platforms from Intel as well as from ARM licensees Qualcomm, NVIDIA, and Texas Instruments.

The company actually had two events that day, one in the morning and then the big showing at the Consumer Electronics Show (CES) keynote.

At that time, I was still getting my feet wet as a member of the tech press and I wasn't invited to attend the first unveiling of Windows running on ARM. But, with a bit of persistence—I just walked through the front door of the briefing room when the PR team overseeing the event wasn't looking—I was there when Microsoft unveiled that Windows was ready for the next generation of computing. But what was missing was the hardware vendor that would take the risk and ship a device running Windows on ARM.

The stage was set for Microsoft to make a big splash in hardware. The company was working on a new operating system called Windows 8 that would make Windows touch-friendly, its hardware partners were gearing up to make devices that ran SoC configurations for smaller and thinner devices, and NVIDIA, Qualcomm, and Texas Instruments were working on ARM hardware at a feverish pace.

But this time would be different; Microsoft had learned from a decade earlier that building a Tablet PC has many challenges and that its experience in this space was going to make it easy to move swiftly and with confidence. The company had a blueprint for how to build a successful product, and it was going to use this knowledge to move ambitiously to compete with Apple and Google.

With the hardware and software story coming together, on paper at least, all Microsoft had to do was execute proficiently. After all, this was Microsoft, and it could buy its way into the market like it had done previously with Xbox. And it already had excellent brand recognition too. This should be easy, right?

———————————————————

For several years, I have been wanting to write the Surface story. As soon as it became apparent that the brand would survive its initial challenges, the narrative of how Microsoft was constructing its next billion-dollar brand was unfolding in broad daylight.

With the help of nearly two-dozen interviews and more than a decade of attending Microsoft events, this is the story of Surface.

Chapter 2 - From Table to Tablet

"We had the vision and the skills to execute, it was a terrific project."

When he was still active at the company he had co-founded, Bill Gates would frequently write memos, known as Gates Notes, that were prized by journalists who were looking to better understand where the company was headed. It was in one of these notes that Gates stated that eventually, every plane would become a computing surface. And with that, a brand idea was born.

Of course, at that time, Microsoft had no idea what Surface would become. The company was just starting to work on building a smart table at the time, but more than a decade later, that brand would prove to be immensely valuable for Microsoft as its strategy shifted. Since then, Surface has played a big role in the success of the company's hardware initiatives.

Building a display that could recognize many different users simultaneously interacting with the hardware was one of the many challenges that Microsoft faced with the Surface table. Today, this type of functionality is well-understood, but back in the mid-2000s, it was bleeding edge technology. Making it work it allowed Microsoft to pioneer new display technologies; when the Surface table shipped, it could support up to 52 simultaneous touch points.

The first generation table had rear Digital Light Processing (DLP) projection cameras, an Intel Core 2 Duo processor, Radeon X1650 graphics, and 2GB of DDR2 RAM; these were high-end specifications for the time. And their inclusion in the product helps explain why the device cost $10,000. Also, anyone intending to move this hardware would need to enlist the help of a friend or three, as it weighed 198 pounds.

The Surface table was sold as a complete solution where Microsoft controlled the hardware and software experiences of a device that would eventually point it down the road of building its own PCs.

First Generation Surface table

The first Surface table was unveiled by Steve Ballmer on May 30, 2007. Adoption was slow but consistent, and large companies like T-Mobile, AT&T, and Harrah's were among the first to gamble on the product.

But Microsoft's primary goal with the Surface table was to help push experiences that combined software and hardware in new ways. In a world where things were either analog or digital, the Surface table was designed to blend or even blur this divide by allowing physical objects to be placed on the display and then be interacted both physically and digitally.

This capability was the Surface table's biggest selling point: it could recognize more than touch input, it also could recognize objects. For corporations, it was a conversation piece and showcased that they were "forward thinkers" as they were early adopters of new technology.

With the perspective of history, we can see now that the Surface table was the first Mixed Reality (MR) device that the company had ever created, though that term wasn't used at the time. To this day, Microsoft is still exploring this space with devices like its HoloLens and Windows Mixed Reality headsets. But the Surface table was the first to reach commercial availability.

The technical success of the Surface table was critical for Microsoft's long-term ambitions to be a bigger player in hardware. It proved that, given the time and resources, the company could build something truly unique and that this could be a big factor in the long-term success of the brand.

But Surface was less successful financially; Microsoft did build a second version, announced in January of 2011, with the help of Samsung. Known as the Samsung SUR40, this second-generation Surface table was priced at $8,400 and weighed only 80 pounds.

With this second generation Surface table, Microsoft introduced a new screen technology called PixelSense that replaced the cameras in the original with a more sophisticated way to detect objects placed on the display. This name stuck. Microsoft would eventually rebrand the tables as PixelSense devices as the company was secretly building other hardware and wanted to use the Surface brand for its upcoming tablets.

Even though the SUR40 was the last of its kind, the experience of building the device allowed Microsoft to better understand the critical aspects of building hardware. Everything from creating high-end displays, the manufacturing process, and of course, delivering the software was better understood after this product was built.

And all of this knowledge would become a foundation for Microsoft's big hardware bet, trying to become a premium player in the PC market.

Chapter 3 - Building the First

"Our partners were chasing margins, not innovation"

For a software giant like Microsoft, getting into the hardware business was not something to be undertaken lightly. Doing so takes time. It takes a substantial amount of money. And most importantly, it requires execution.

Microsoft also had to consider its PC maker partners. The company had for decades depended on third-party companies to build the hardware that ran its operating system and other software. To suddenly change that relationship would cause anxiety across the ecosystem.

Because of this anxiety, Surface nearly didn't happen. Steve Ballmer, who was then Microsoft's CEO, and Bill Gates disagreed about the need to build hardware. The two, at times, had heated arguments about whether the company should go down this path. If it were not for Ballmer's belief that Microsoft needed to build its own hardware and his willingness to push back against Gates and the company's board, the Surface PC product line would never have existed.

The Microsoft board argued that there was no need to make this investment and that the company should continue helping its PC maker partners create new hardware that pushed Windows forward. But Ballmer argued that only Microsoft had the software and hardware teams that could actually compete against Apple. And that if Microsoft didn't act immediately, the PC could be displaced by the rising tide of Cupertino.

To many at the time, the idea of Microsoft building its own hardware seemed illogical. The company was doing well selling its

Windows solution via computers offered by the likes of HP, Lenovo, Dell, and many others. But others could sense a big change coming. Ballmer was among them, and he was able to convince the board that touch-based PCs were the future of computing.

The problem was that selling this touch-based future to its partners was not an easy task. So Microsoft needed to show the world that it could build a touch-based computer that everyone would love: the company would try to do this with Windows 8, but there was a small caveat.

While this new product line was not a "bet the company" project, as Microsoft had many streams of revenue, it was a still huge risk to the well-established and highly-profitable Windows business unit. The board told Ballmer that it was supportive of him as long as Windows, the brand, would not be hurt by a failed attempt by Microsoft to build its own PC hardware.

It's impossible to talk about the building of the Surface brand without diving into the development of Windows 8 and, more specifically, the team that was building this operating system. Coming off the success of Windows 7, Windows chief Steven Sinofsky was firing on all cylinders and now it was time for a big bet.

Microsoft had known all along that after Windows 7, it would take a chance with Windows 8 and focus on making it touch-friendly. It could see how the market would eventually move into what it called a "touch-first" world, as was the case with the smartphone. And it wanted to position Windows 8 as the premier desktop operating system to showcase this emerging technology.

In addition to building Windows 8 for traditional CPUs and PCs, Microsoft was also building a version of the product for the mobile device-focused ARM platform as well. Windows on ARM (WOA) was secretly being developed so it could be be showcased at CES 2011, and it represented a new direction for Microsoft. While the company had partnerships with Intel and AMD, the company had long desired to bring ARM into its ecosystem and felt that after the success of Windows 7, the timing was right.

But it's not possible to use off-the-shelf computers to showcase the future of computing when you are building a new operating system for a new type of input and a new CPU. So Microsoft needed a device that would work well for both scenarios, with touch, and with traditional PC input types.

This initiative was backed by Sinofsky, who helped to bring together the software and hardware teams that would be needed and took on the challenge of bringing both products to life. Of course, he was not alone: there were many players here such as Julie Larson-Green, Panos Panay, Gabe Aul, Jensen Harris, Ralf Groene, Stevie Bathiche and many, many more who deserve recognition for their efforts to modernize Windows and make Surface a reality.

The early days of Surface PC development were treated like a skunkworks project at Microsoft. There was absolute secrecy for the lucky few who were selected to work on the project and they were told to keep the assignment secret from their families and friends. On Microsoft's campus, nearly everyone who wasn't involved was kept in the dark. And even C-suite executives were often not included in crucial decisions.

It was this secrecy that created the "tenting" process at Microsoft. This controversial way of screening people before working on Surface hardware created a rift between employees about who is in the club and who is not. To be tented, you are subjected to a series of interviews to see if you could be trusted with company secrets.

The tenting procedures also included training that told employees how to better hide the tasks they were working on: not putting code names in subject lines or opening slide decks in public places. There are many different levels of tenting as well with each project getting its own tent and you are only "tented" into projects as necessary.

The process is designed to be intimidating by scaring the employee into not leaking content to other Microsoft employees or outside parties. Microsoft treated the process as if you were receiving a government security clearance. Intimidation tactics were used to vet those who should not be authorized with the sensitive information.

And there was an urban legend on the Microsoft campus that at some level of tenting, you would meet with a former CIA employee before you got clearance. If this process did exist, he/she is not very good at their job based on what I and other reporters have uncovered about Surface over the years.

Sinofsky and team kept the hardware and software behind several layers of security at the company's Redmond campus. To say that there was paranoia around leaks for either the touch interface for Windows or the Surface leaking would be a significant understatement.

An engineer working on the touch UI told me that one day, late after work, he was having a beer at a local brewery talking with other employees who were not on the project and accidentally mentioned the word "Metro"—the name for Microsoft's modern UI at the time—and he excused himself to the restroom where he began vomiting. He thought he may have accidentally ruined the Windows 8 and Surface PC announcements by simply saying one word about the user interface.

Sinofsky always had a bit of a reputation inside of Microsoft. On one side, people considered him a "cut above" everyone else. He was smart, had a way of getting things done, and helped streamline development of Windows at a time when the company was highly political and also quite siloed.

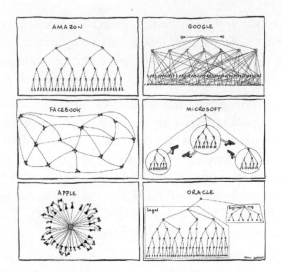

There is a tongue-in-cheek org chart comparison created by Manu Cornet of Bonkersworld.net that shows Microsoft as a bunch of silos with guns pointed at each other. This was uncomfortably realistic to those inside the company. Every organization within Microsoft was indeed fighting for themselves at that time and not working with other organizations. One person said that Sinofsky wasn't holding a gun but rather a rocket launcher, and that if he didn't like you, he would take you and your entire project down in flames.

Sinofsky was a classic micromanager. He was good at letting people do what they excelled at but he also felt the need to be entirely in charge of the operation. He also didn't play well with others; other managers disliked him and he wasn't exactly great at building cross-organizational relationships.

In meetings, even with senior leadership, if someone asked him a question that he felt was below him or he thought the person was being lazy, he would not respond and sit in silence, creating an awkward pause in a meeting. For all of his good ideas and intentions, he undermined his ability to accomplish what needed to be done by making too many enemies with others inside Microsoft.

When Sinofsky was approached by Frank Shaw, Microsoft's communications chief, to assist him in launching Windows 8 and the Surface line, Sinofsky turned down this help in favor of controlling the entire process himself. Sinofsky wasn't interested in sharing the spotlight, and he wasn't interested in other people's ideas.

With the level of secrecy around the new Surface PC line and the development of Windows 8, the teams building the hardware and software became a close-knit operation. There was a lot of trust, and leaks on the hardware side were nearly zero during most of the project. On the software side, leaks were minimal: Only serious enthusiasts were learning anything about Windows 8 development with apps like "Red Pill" that could alter the Windows Registry to reveal some secret and unannounced features.

During this time, Panay and his Surface team were busy building two products, Surface RT—based on the ARM platform—and Surface Pro, which was a more traditional Intel-based tablet PC. The initial goal was to have them launch at the same time. But because of delays in Surface Pro development, it was decided that the RT iteration would launch alongside Windows 8 in late 2012 and that the Pro version would follow three months later, in early 2013.

Sinofsky had a chip on his shoulder. When Apple announced the iPad two years earlier, that company was praised for releasing a large touchscreen device with support for multitouch gestures.

The problem? Microsoft and Sinofsky had been working on these technologies for a couple of years before the iPad was announced. But he wasn't able to show the world what the company was capable of creating until after the iPad had already shipped and he was afraid of being accused of copying Cupertino's ideas.

Sinofsky had tried to undermine the iPad and slyly promote Microsoft's work by showing off a 10.6-inch "development station" running a touchscreen version of Windows at the AllThingsD conference in June of 2011. The fact that the Surface RT and Surface Pro both launched with 10.6-inch touchscreens over a year later was not coincidental.

Microsoft had quietly shown the world what it viewed as a touch-first device but no one had put together the pieces that the company would eventually launch its own tablets too.

Back inside of Microsoft, with Windows 8's new touch UI shown to the world about a year ahead of the release of the Surface, Panay and his team worked feverishly trying to figure out how their hardware would fit into the world of computers.

How could they differentiate the hardware to make sure that it stood out? What ports were needed for a device that was going to hopefully be the best tablet and laptop the world had ever seen?

There was also in-fighting occurring on multiple levels regarding how to market the device. The Surface Pro was an easy device, it was a PC that ran everything you know about Windows in a different form factor. But the Surface RT, which was running the soon-to-be-named Windows RT, had serious limitations.

And there was another problem: time was moving too quickly. Sinofsky and Panay both knew that the first generation Surface devices were unlikely to change the world overnight. But they were still hopeful that Surface would push Microsoft and the industry in a new direction. And with only so many hours in a day and needing time to prepare for a release, decisions had to be made.

Early Surface Pro Mockup

Developing a kickstand is said to be one of Panay's and his team's bigger wins for the first generation Surface RT and Pro. The early Surface Pro mockup shows how the company was rapidly prototyping the design using basic materials to better understand how this form factor would function in the real world.

At a time when hardware was largely the same from nearly every manufacturer, Surface represented the first break from the common laptop mold to challenge both traditional laptops and tablets.

The first Surface RT kickstand only had one stop point at 22 degrees, though Panay and his team did not want this. They were pushing for a multi-position kickstand for the first generation but ran out of time and were unable to reliably manufacture a device that supported this feature. And as the calendar kept turning over, day by day, a line had to be drawn in the sand.

When the team completed the first generation of hardware, they didn't meet all of their objectives and Panay knew that they were far from done. But deadlines had to be met as the marriage of a software release and the hardware's completion had to align.

And there was the other issue of what to name the product; building it is one thing but creating a sustainable brand name is not something you can spin up overnight. Microsoft already owned the Surface brand name, but there was some pushback at this time about using that name because some thought that one day they would build another table..

There is one another thing to consider with the Surface name. Microsoft knew that journalists frequently browsed through the company's trademark applications and that by using a brand name it already owned, it could easily maintain the secrecy around the development of the brand. Less paperwork, fewer places for its plans to leak out. Surface was the perfect name.

The final task for naming the hardware was the order of the words Microsoft, Surface, Windows, and RT. This may sound inconsequential but in the giant cogs of a company the size of Microsoft, some details are analyzed to death. And the naming of Surface RT is a great example. . And of course, there was also the Surface Pro being developed at this time, and it would also need to be named.

The company went through many iterations, including Surface for Windows RT, Surface with Windows RT, and Microsoft Surface for RT. Surface Pro went through similar iterations like Surface for Windows 8 Pro and Microsoft Surface for Windows 8 Pro. But as the clock pushed up against the 12th hour, Microsoft Surface RT and Microsoft Surface Pro were the names chosen.

But even after the names were agreed upon, there was more to the story.

At this point in time, Microsoft had an image problem. Microsoft wasn't "cool" when compared to Apple, Google, or any of the younger companies. Sinofsky and others argued that the name "Microsoft" should not be included in the product's announcement to make the hardware stand out. Similar to how Xbox is never called

Microsoft Xbox, there was a vision that this device, when it was announced, should just be Surface and not have the branding of the company on the hardware.

Despite their best efforts, Ballmer was insistent on it being a Microsoft product and as the final sign-offs were being completed, the hardware was approved for mass production with a Microsoft logo on the back.

Chapter 4 - Inviting the World

"Secrecy is fun, right up until it is not"

With the design and development of the first Surface PCs nearly complete, Sinofsky, Panay, Michael Angiulo, and a few others at Microsoft began preparing for the announcement. Despite Sinofsky not wanting him at the event, Steve Ballmer insisted that he have a role in the reveal. And since he was the CEO, it was impossible to say no.

The teams put in an immense amount of time and effort to make the announcement run as smoothly as possible. Panay alone put in hundreds of hours to ensure that his delivery was perfect. But others complained that Sinofsky, who did participate in practice sessions, did not rehearse as much Panay did when preparing for the presentation.

During interviews for this book, several people spoke about how Panay is what they called a coachable leader. That is, he knew the direction he needed to go but was open to help on how he would get there.

For example, while some may use tape to mark an "X" on the floor to denote where to stand and which direction to face, Panay would instead count the ideal number of steps to take to get to a location on the stage, ensuring that it felt natural and not rushed. He would test, retest, and get feedback on how and where he should stand and the direction he should be facing.

For those who knew him, this was nothing new. But those on the outside watching him and his team get ready for this first Surface

PC reveal felt that they could see the passion manifesting itself as the clock continued to tick forward.

After all the secrecy, research, planning, prototyping, and hard work, it was time to announce the device to the outside world. The team decided Ballmer, Sinofsky, Panay, and a few others would present the results of their hard work on June 18th.

Leading up to the launch event, there was a lot of mystery surrounding the devices. Because of the cutthroat secrecy around Windows 8's modern UI and the Surface tablets, the leaks were kept to a minimum. While there were whispers among insiders about how Microsoft was working on *something* for the launch of Windows 8, no one had a clear idea of what to expect except for one Asian publication with a sketchy track record.

In the early 2010s, DigiTimes was known for its wild predictions about hardware coming off the manufacturing lines and it was pumping out rumors for nearly every company in the industry. Most notably, it made predictions about Apple hardware that were cited frequently in western publications and drove millions of page views each month.

This vicious cycle of Apple hardware rumors, and publications writing everything as truth without fact-checking, created the situation we see with most tech industry blogs today. And there was so much noise at this time that it was often hard to discern fact from fiction; while DigiTimes was often wrong, when it came to Microsoft's Surface, it nailed the prediction.

Six months prior to the announcement of the Surface RT and Pro tablets, DigiTimes reported that Microsoft would make its own PC hardware.

One of the other rare leaks that occurred prior to announcement came from Panay himself. While working on the assembly process with partners in China, he posted a picture to social media that seemed innocent enough. The picture did not have any revealing information but he forgot to turn off the geotagging and industry observers saw that he was in a part of the world that was known for producing laptops and smartphones.

At that time, it seemed unlikely that Microsoft would build a PC because of its vast ecosystem of PC maker partners. And besides, these partners had all the expertise right? Why would Microsoft venture into new territory when it could simply depend on these partners to pick up the pace, build their own premium PCs, and save Microsoft from making unnecessary capital investments?

But Microsoft had its reasons. A resurgent Apple was releasing successful products like the MacBook Air and the MacBook Pro, the latter of which was then being upgraded with high-end Retina displays. Apple's advantage was that it controlled the hardware *and* the software. And this gave them a leg up in development when compared to Microsoft and its partners.

Put more generally, Microsoft felt that it needed to control its own destiny. The writing was on the wall, and personal computing was shifting from traditional desktop and laptop PCs to a more modern and mobile computing paradigm. So while the company's mobile efforts continued to falter, Microsoft was not going to let that happen to the PC business. It had to ship its own hardware.

For many years, Microsoft maintained a big presence at industry events where it would announce new products, as it had done at CES 2011. But for the Surface reveal, the company decided that it wanted the stage all to itself, and it chose a venue in Los Angeles.

In a bid to maintain secrecy, Microsoft's invitation to press was rather cryptic. Typically, the company would give journalists and bloggers some insight about what to expect. But for this event, they were simply told was to go to Los Angeles; the subject of the event was not disclosed in advance. Nor was the event location.

Further, unlike previous invites from Microsoft and other companies, where one typically gets two weeks or more to prepare, the media was told about this event only four days in advance.

The invites for this secret event were sent out on June 14th with the announcement date on the 18th. For those who were traveling from out of town, Microsoft requested that they fly to a city, for an event they would say nothing about, at a location that was not being disclosed.

As the four-day window contracted, small bits of information began to leak out. Reporter Ina Fried penned a post on AllThingsD claiming that Microsoft would discuss Windows RT, a version of Windows 8 designed for ARM chips, but she did not state that the company would be launching its own hardware.

Being on the outside, I remember looking everywhere for clues about what Microsoft would announce and where they would likely host this event. But Microsoft successfully kept much of the information about the hardware a secret to the outside world until they were ready to show it off.

There weren't any patents showing up online and Microsoft's web assets didn't show up early, as they had in the past, spoiling previous events. And everyone working on the project managed to keep the information secret. Looking back, this was one of the best-kept secrets in Microsoft's recent history, and it set a high watermark for keeping upcoming products out of the public's eye until they were ready to be shown off.

Adding to the drama, the announcement location was complicated by another Microsoft conference, the Windows Phone Summit, which was being held on June 20th in San Francisco. At the time of this event, I had been recently hired as the Managing Editor for Neowin, a Microsoft-focused blog, I had assigned the Windows Phone Summit to my good friend Andy Weir, who was en-route to San Francisco after a few stops in the U.S. for other events when the invites went out.

This triggered some panicked calls to Microsoft to see if it was worth having Weir take a flight over to Los Angeles for the mystery event. Their recommendation, of course, was that he should attend even though they would not say where exactly it would be held. A few hundred dollars down the drain for an additional flight and few more for a hotel and Weir was on his way.

Even though there are many journalists in the LA area who could cover the launch, for those who followed Microsoft closely, attending both the mystery event and the Windows Phone Summit was a complicated dance as each promised information about the company's future.

To make life easier, Microsoft could have hosted both events in the same city, and possibly at different venues. But insiders tell me that the secrecy of the development of the hardware and Windows 8, and Sinofsky's disdain for the Windows Phone group, led to the decision to not host the events in the same city.

After many loud complaints from the press who were waiting in Los Angeles not knowing where to go, Microsoft eventually revealed that the announcement would be held at Milk Studios.

The race began to get an early look at the venue where the company would make an announcement that would forever change the course of the industry. The marketing team dotted the surrounding landscape with hieroglyphics, or what seemed like ancient encryption drawings, as this was the first look at the Surface hardware; these images inspired the cover design of this book.

Inside the studio was a stage at the center of the room, surrounded by chairs, with a large screen behind the presenter. It was minimalistic in nature, reminiscent of how Apple presented its products. And as the lights came up, Steve Ballmer strolled out on stage, ready to announce a major change in Microsoft's plans for the future.

Chapter 5 - Surface Unveiling

"We had no idea the vicious cycle we were about to kick off"

In a dark hanger at Milk Studios in Los Angeles, stood a stage with a blue backdrop. Microsoft security was heavy, and marketing people were fluttering around the room like butterflies trying to make sure everything was perfect. And then the lights came up as Steve Ballmer walked on to the stage.

If you haven't ever seen Ballmer present, he is loud and bombastic, and he was passionate about everything that Microsoft was doing at that time. He commanded the stage and the room like a general leading his troops into battle. And his voice acted as the calvary horn to let everyone know that it was time to march forward.

Ballmer wanted to attend the event because he didn't want the Surface launch to offend Microsoft's partners. Microsoft is a company that leans heavily on its partners. From building PCs to selling its cloud services, Microsoft would not be where it is today without its vast partner ecosystem. So with the software giant about to announce a new computer that *would* compete with its partners, Ballmer wanted to explain that his company had been making hardware devices for decades. And that's exactly what he did.

Walking through everything from Microsoft's first mouse to the Xbox 360 with Kinect, Ballmer demonstrated to the world and its PC maker partners that this was simply another part of the Microsoft equation and not an attack on their businesses.

Ballmer believed that the release of the Surface was similar to that of the first mouse. This was an important comparison, and to some extent, one might agree with that sentiment. Surface did help make touch-screen PCs ubiquitous and its existence didn't stop other PC makers from creating similar PCs.

Ballmer spent about 11 minutes on stage, but only 60 seconds of that time dedicated to Surface RT. While he did show the product briefly, he quickly handed things over to Sinofsky.

Knowing that Sinofsky would have preferred that Ballmer not be there at all, Ballmer's short time on stage starts to make more sense. His part of the presentation was brief: Come out, set the context, announce the product but tell the audience virtually nothing about it, and then hand it over to Sinofsky.

Jogging onto the stage, Sinofsky immediately took control of the conversation away from Ballmer. It's is customary when a presentation changes hands for one or both colleagues to say "thanks" or something of that nature. But that didn't happen here. Looking back, one can feel the disdain that Sinofsky had for Ballmer being on that stage.

Like an animatronic in a Disney World ride, Sinofsky abruptly stopped jogging as he was about to begin and then reset his position, every so slightly, then dove into announcing the product. There were no pleasantries, no attempts at connecting with the audience. Just a deep dive right into the pitch explaining why this product was going to change everything.

In an early segment of the presentation that would foreshadow the level of future success that the hardware would experience, the demonstration came off the rails. While attempting to use the Windows RT's web browser, the device locked up. Sinofsky tried for a few awkward seconds to revive it with no luck.

Using a backup Surface RT, Sinofsky continued the presentation without many other hiccups. And the world got its first look at the hardware that Panay and his team had been building for years by this point. In addition to the Surface RT, Microsoft also announced the Touch Cover, a 3-mm thin cover for the Surface line that used a touch-sensitive material to create a flat keyboard that Microsoft claimed was faster and more comfortable than typing on glass.

Surface RT with Touch Cover

Microsoft also announced the Surface Pro, its first traditional Intel-based PC. It would eventually be a home run after a few iterations, but like the Surface RT, it initially had trouble as well.

Microsoft's Michael Angiulo walked out on to the stage next, thanked Sinofsky for the introduction, and then showed off Surface for Windows 8 Pro, as the product was originally and ponderously called. Pitched as a powerful PC for those who design and create things, Surface Pro featured a high-end Intel CPU, perimeter venting, and the same kickstand as the RT. But it was, in all ways, a "real" PC, unlike Surface RT, which ran Windows RT and was restricted in terms of performance and applications compatibility.

First Generation Surface Pro

One thing worth pointing out from this first public introduction to Surface Pro is how far digital inking has come since then. While the first ink demos with Surface Pro and Surface Pen were cutting edge at the time, you can see a significant amount of latency, a lag between the pen tip and what was written on-screen—Microsoft would eventually refine with future iterations of the products.

Microsoft also showed off a more traditional typing cover for both Surface PCs called the Type Cover. As history would soon show, consumers did not like the Touch Cover and Microsoft quickly discontinued that product with the Type Cover and its traditional keyboard experience becoming the must-have accessory for the Surface line.

And it was at this time that Panay made his first appearance on what would eventually become his stage for the rest of the Surface history. It was an awkward beginning.

After Angiulo announced the Type Cover, he asked to have the entire Surface product line brought on stage, and specifically asked for "Panos" to come out with the multiple colors of the Touch Cover.

Sinofsky carried Surface RT and Angiulo held aloft Surface Pro for the audience

Sinofsky exited the stage after a brief and half-hearted round of applause. But Angiulo continued the awkwardness by tapping Panay on the shoulder as he tried to leave the Type Covers he had been modeling on a nearby table. "Panos Panay is the leader of the team that created Surface," Anguio revealed. "And he has some great stories ... about how the product came to be."

Being the 4th of 4 people to appear on stage that day may not have seemed like a big deal at the time. But for Panay, this was his entry into the limelight as the person behind the hardware. And while this was a defining moment in his career, not long after, he would be the only one making all the key Surface announcements.

Like any good conductor, Panay paid homage to the entire team. This wasn't a singular achievement, he said, but was the work of many, including key players such as Ralf Groene and Stevie Bathiche.

His time on stage was spent talking in-depth about the hardware and demonstrating the Touch Cover, one of the first Surface products that Microsoft would discontinue. But the stage was set, not for just Surface, but for Panay as well. He would be an integral part of the brand, the face of Surface.

From the very beginning, no matter what happened with the release of these first devices, Panay was saying internally that he needed three iterations for this product line. In hindsight this was obvious. But at the time, the vision was set but the challenges ahead were immense.

With the first generation of hardware announced, the entire team could begin to breathe again as the world became aware of what they were working on.

When they returned to Microsoft's campus, the Surface team found that they were the cool kids on the block. Everyone at the Redmond-based company wanted to see, touch, feel, and contribute to the project. Despite a few hiccups, and not a little awkwardness, the Surface launch had gone smoothly and the company's efforts at secrecy had paid off. But the work was far from complete.

Thanks to the onstage issues with Windows RT, Sinofsky was not thrilled with his performance. He prided himself on perfection, but the software had come up short in front of the world. The operating system crashing was an embarrassing snafu for a company that was launching new hardware running a new operating system. And even though Microsoft still had months to polish things up, the stress of launching an incomplete product began to build.

First impressions matter. And while the hardware looked spectacular, the software's true colors were beginning to show. Even though this should have been a time of celebration for the company, the truth is that the real work was only starting and the road ahead would be far from smooth.

Chapter 6 - A Perfect Disaster

"We hit every pothole on the road and dug a few more too"

If you are looking for the perfect example of how you don't want a product release to go, look no further than Windows 8 and Surface RT.

After the June announcement of the new line of Surface tablets that Microsoft was building, Sinofsky and his team were put on pedestals inside the company. Finally, after years of secrecy, everyone at Microsoft knew what was happening behind closed doors and it seemed like most of them wanted to help make this project a success.

The problem was that they had little time to do so. While Windows 8 was well understood and its touch-centric design was critical to the operating system, building apps and scenarios specifically for Surface was proving to be difficult as the cutoff date for shipping the software and hardware was rapidly approaching.

One of the key aspects of both Windows 8 and RT was the introduction of the app store, called the Windows Store. But it was even more important to Windows RT because the Windows Store was the only way you could install applications on that system. Windows RT, inexplicably, was incompatible with the vast array of desktop applications that made Windows so popular; it was, as critics noted, the first Windows version that was incompatible with Windows applications.

But with Apple's mobile app store booming, Microsoft thought that it could ride that wave. And as we all know now, just because you build it, doesn't mean people will show up.

Critics of this system included many of Microsoft's own employees. Because of Sinofsky's hostile approach, he was alienating himself from the company's other business organizations. And despite mandates from management to build applications, internal politics was winning. Business owners were only slowly supporting Sinofsky's store.

Two people who worked at Microsoft at this time noted that they did help Windows build new apps, but they did the absolute minimum required to support the new touch interface. One said that Sinofsky had personally attacked his team during a meeting and that he made building a touch application a low priority for his division as a result. Why help out the guy who was trying to undermine his agenda?

The infighting at Microsoft around this time was reaching its peak. On one side, you had Sinofsky clamoring for more power and on the other, you had hardware and software teams under different leadership trying to work together to build a new product. It wasn't a case of having too many cooks in the kitchen, it was like the sous chefs actively burning food to undermine the other chefs.

Windows 8 featured a Start screen that replaced the familiar Start menu

The downfall of Windows 8, with its touch-first user interface and unfamiliar Start screen, represented a turning point for Windows and for Microsoft as a company.

When someone turned on a Surface for the first time, there were no on-screen clues to show them how to navigate or use the system. Instead of providing a helpful tutorial, often referred to as an "Out-of-Box-Experience", or OOBE for short, Microsoft shipped Windows 8 blind to customers who had to then learn the new environment with little or no help.

And by removing the Start button, which had been in every version of Windows since Windows 95, and replacing it with "hot corners," the user was left struggling to figure out how to, well, *start*. The OS was trying to move in a bold new direction but failed on execution and user education.

Windows 8 desktop with the missing Start button

Early reviews of Windows 8 lambasted Microsoft for its hidden, non-discoverable gestures. Peter Bright of Ars Technica noted that "it's not that it didn't work; it's just that it wasn't very obvious." This proved to be a critical flaw for both the hardware and the software.

Paul Thurrott, then with Windows IT Pro, said that Windows 8 was "the biggest and most confusing upgrade that Microsoft has ever wrought on its most core of platforms," and Tom Warren of the Verge stated, "There's a steep learning curve here." It was clear that Windows 8 was as hostile to its own users as Sinofsky was to the rest of Microsoft. And Microsoft had failed on nearly every aspect of trying to make Windows a modern, touch-friendly platform.

And that was just the software. The marketing was a confusing mess too, and that set up the hardware up for failure.

Specifically, you had Windows RT, which looked like a duck, quacked like a duck, and walked like a duck, but was in fact, a pigeon. Despite last-minute efforts to try and hastily educate the consumer, not being able to run apps downloaded from the Internet proved to be a huge point of friction: Windows RT looked exactly like Windows 8 but it was severely limited in its functionality; consumers were confused.

From the very beginning, the hardware team behind the Surface product line felt that it would take multiple generations, or re-visions, of the devices to reach the success they had envisioned. The early announcement, which was met with great enthusiasm, gave the company hope that its hardware dreams would quickly materialize into the next billion-dollar business for the company. But those high notes would be short-lived.

Remember, this was before the tragedy of Windows 8 was fully understood. But the hardware, at least briefly, was attracting a lot of attention.

For the release, Microsoft hosted a splashy press event in New York City and the company set up a temporary store in the heart of Times Square where it began selling the devices at midnight. There were long lines and tightly controlled security as early adopters– and a few Microsoft employees and their families—waited to play with and possibly buy the hardware. Early indications were that this hardware might actually be a hit for Microsoft.

But after the last streamer fell to the ground, and the sun rose the next day, life moved forward. And a grim new reality was starting to set in.

Reviews of Surface RT were relatively positive. Microsoft's built-in kickstand was a good addition to a tablet, the screen was responsive but colors were a bit muted, battery life was acceptable, and the device certainly felt premium. Looking just at the hardware, the Surface RT was a solid first entry from Microsoft. But outside factors undercut its success from day one.

When Surface RT first went on sale, Microsoft limited its availability to its own retail and online stores in the US and Canada. This was a significant hindrance: many consumers did not live close to a company store and buying a tablet sight-unseen with a new OS that wasn't receiving good reviews was a huge challenge.

Internally, this was a point of contention. The hardware team wanted this device sold in traditional stores too, but Steve Ballmer had other ideas. Microsoft was heavily investing in building out its retail locations, and Ballmer wanted to use the Surface RT as a way to attract customers. This may have been a good idea theoretically, but it failed at its objectives.

The issue was that Microsoft stores had significantly lower foot traffic than traditional electronics retailers. And Surface RT didn't change that: consumers didn't go out of their way to see the new hardware because Microsoft wasn't perceived as a "cool" company like Apple. And with Windows 8 off to a dismal start, Surface RT was further undercut in a classic case of mismanagement.

Would the device have sold better if it was initially available at Best Buy, Staples, and other retail shops around the US? It certainly wouldn't have sold less, that's for sure.

And then there was the confusing message, This device ran a

system that looked like Windows 8 and had Office applications pre-installed, but it couldn't run desktop applications downloaded from the web. If you couldn't find an app in the store, and you couldn't because the selection was dismal, then you were out of luck.

None of this was a surprise to those who built the product. Most agreed that the hardware was good, but the overall experience was significantly underwhelming. And after the midnight launch, insiders watched the sales figures trickle in and the news was not good. In the first week after release, it was clear that Microsoft had manufactured too many devices.

Windows 8 and Windows RT were both disasters, but it doesn't matter if software sits unsold. Microsoft had a bigger problem: What to do with all the metal that was sitting in warehouses losing value with each passing day?

Even though Surface Pro launched three months after Windows RT and received less attention from the press, it sold far better than the RT. But the launch of the Pro was marred by its own issues. In this case, miscommunication.

Microsoft formally and accidentally announced the launch of Surface Pro at CES 2013 in Las Vegas. Ahead of the conference, Microsoft was preparing to tell the press the details about the Surface Pro's release date and other bits of information but under embargo; meaning they would be briefed at the event but could not publish information until a later date.

But not everyone at Microsoft got the memo. Some publications were told they had to hold their information and others were told they could publish that day.

Not surprisingly, those who were not held to an embargo immediately posted what they had learned online. Chaos ensued. Microsoft had to make a choice: Ask those writers to retract their posts or lift the embargo for everyone.

Because you can't really erase anything from the Internet, Microsoft decided to let all of the publications it had briefed to start posting the content. But some publications became angry at Microsoft because they had not been briefed yet. And a few that had been briefed had not written anything yet because they thought they had more time to write. To say that many angry words were exchanged via email and phone between reporters and Microsoft would be an understatement.

Surface Pro was going to fix what everyone didn't like about Surface RT. But with its botched release with the press and its availability coming right after the holiday shopping season, Microsoft had pushed this hardware out of the door on a broken leg.

Chapter 7 - The Writedown

"We all knew it was coming but we didn't think it would be this bad."

After the launch of Surface RT and Windows 8, the reality that was quietly being whispered around Microsoft's offices was coming to fruition. Sales of the hardware and operating system were not meeting expectations internally. And the reviews were not helping the situation.

But what made the launch different than that of Windows Vista, Microsoft's least-well-received version of Windows to date, was that it could not be fixed with a software update. In warehouses across the United States, Microsoft had Surface RTs stockpiled like war rations except there was never going to be a war and there was no enemy other than time.

And piled high they were. Microsoft manufactured more than 4 million Windows RT tablets and had about 3 million sitting in warehouses. It also had piles of accessories that were not selling either.

Every day the hardware team would get updates on the sales progress of the device. And while the numbers were initially in the thousands, not long after the release, those figures dwindled. On some days in the first quarter of availability, there were less than a hundred units sold across the country and the realization that this device would not be a success was quickly manifesting itself in heated management meetings.

The company needed a new strategy. This growing failure was part of a sobering and on-going lesson for Microsoft, that it was no longer the dominant force in the industry, and that consumers were choosing other platforms.

But the company did try to generate some noise after the release. Microsoft released several commercials with one, called "Movement," that executives hoped would become a viral hit and help put the Surface brand into the minds of consumers as they looked to purchase a tablet.

Some will remember this now infamous commercial by the dancing school girls and clicking of the Surface covers. At the time, it was Microsoft's attempt to launch a new brand and this commercial, for both good and bad, grabbed a bit of attention but unfortunately did not help sales. Most simply mocked it.

While the company had hoped that the Surface RT would drive traffic to its stores, week-to-week traffic reports showed that the device was having little impact. With Surface Pro still several months away, Microsoft finally decided to get the tablet to where the customers were actually shopping, Best Buy and Staples.

In the second week of December, the two retailers started offering a version of the device with 32GB of storage, but with no keyboard cover, for $499. There was also a version with a touch keyboard cover for $599; a 64 GB version with keyboard cover cost $699.

The problem was that this was too little, too late; the holiday shopping season was nearing its completion with only two weeks of availability at these critical locations.

But there was an even bigger problem for Microsoft. In the haste to get these devices to other retail establishments, there was no time for training the employees who were selling these products to consumers. They often didn't know the difference between Windows 8 and Windows RT. Worse for Microsoft, Best Buy wasn't ready for the devices. The hardware was shoved into any place where the stores could find the room; in some cases, the devices showed up in the PC section of stores, and in others, they might be found in the mobile phone section.

With employees telling customers incorrect information (apps could be installed from outside the store), a half-baked OS that was confusing to use, and a price that was too high, the Surface RT had one of the highest return rates in Best Buy's history.

By the end of the holiday shopping season, the trend was clear, Surface RT was not going to be a hit. It was quickly turning into a liability as inventory sat aging on store shelves.

Microsoft believed that the price was the biggest obstacle that was holding the consumer back from buying Surface RT. It was not ignorant of the other issues, but the company knew that pricing was the first barrier encountered and by lowering the cost of the device, perhaps it could sell more units.

One thing that gets lost on many who remember this time period is that there is a difference between a write-down and write off. There are some who believed that Microsoft wrote-off the hardware, meaning it cleaned its books of the hardware costs and could then sell the devices at any price. This was not the case. Instead, the company performed a write-down of the value of the hardware, meaning that what it previously said these assets were worth was now significantly less.

The write-down was announced in July 2013 and even insiders were surprised by the figure. At over $900 million, Microsoft was setting the stage for a fire sale of the device. With the write-down, the company was able to cut the price of the device by $150.00 and it did help to move more units.

Before the write-down occurred, if Microsoft sustained its Surface RT sales rate each week, it would have taken about 8 years to clear inventory. And that figure is likely optimistic because as the device continued to age, sales would inevitably slow even further; the write-down was necessary.

For Microsoft, the write-down did more damage to the company's image than the actual fiscal correction. The company was transitioning into a Software-as-a-Service (SaaS) model and Office 365 was starting to take off, but that didn't matter because all the earnings headlines at that time focused on the colossal hardware inventory adjustment.

In an interview with CNN, Panay described the experience as humbling and acknowledged that, internally, it was a really tough time.

Microsoft's goal of creating a premium PC brand was in jeopardy. It had a tablet that was not selling and an OS that was being mocked by its competitors. And all of the press around the brand was negative, to put it lightly.

The company was running a fire-drill to try and move past the calamity of Windows 8 and now, this major write down. For many, this was about as bad as it could get because the Surface team had yet to establish themselves or the Surface brand, Microsoft's core platform, Windows, was failing to adapt to the modern age, and the company's mobile OS, Windows Phone, was failing to generate any tangible momentum for the company.

But Microsoft was well positioned for a fight. Despite a mediocre quarter, the company had a lot of cash in the bank, a wide portfolio of enterprise products that were selling well, and its new SaaS ambitions were starting to show signs of life.

By knocking $150 off the price point of the Surface RT, the company had hoped that this would generate positive noise around the device and increase the sales rate. But its problem were compounded by the fact that the company wanted Surface to be a premium product and by slashing the price, it was inching closer towards becoming yet another 'value' option in the crowded space that its hardware partners dominated with price, scale, and a variety of options.

The goal of the write-down was to clear the warehouses and to that degree, it did. While not always at the new $350 price point, Microsoft did eventually sell all of its Surface RT hardware.

The company offered the device for sale at some of its conferences for as little as $99 and during Black Friday of 2013, Best Buy sold the device for $199. The Black Friday sale was one of the few bright spots for the company. On that single day, it sold over 240,000 units at Best Buy alone.

Before the launch of the RT, Steve Ballmer said "we either built too many or not enough." In hindsight, the answer is easy: Microsoft built far too many and the ramifications of the write-down would impact every generation of hardware released after this device. Microsoft now conservatively orders for new hardware launches as they are deathly afraid of another "hardware inventory correction."

But the road to success is often bumpy, and while this mountain presented serious challenges for Microsoft, the company was not giving up this easily. Ballmer and the Surface team knew that the PC world lacked a "hero" and the company was determined that Microsoft would somehow, some way, become this brand.

The decision to build Surface RT 2 and Surface Pro 2 was an easy choice, and Microsoft couldn't back down. And when the write-down occurred, the company was not only finalizing the second generation of hardware but already had its eyes set on what would become the true savior of the Surface brand, the Surface Pro 3.

Chapter 8 - Chasing Two The Success Dragon

"We hoped that by digging deeper, we could get out of the hole."

When you fall off a bike, you can either sit on the ground crying, or you can get back up and try again. The Surface RT failed miserably on nearly every metric imaginable, but Microsoft wasn't giving up that easily; the company was already working on the second generation of the device when it released the first.

Inside the company, morale was down, and those who worked on the hardware and software had to deal with the ramifications of releasing a flop. While the company tried to turn the tides on the early reception of Windows 8 and the Surface brand, internally the lines dividing Microsoft's organizations were growing deeper.'

After the release of the Surface RT in 2012, being part of the Surface team was seen as a career liability inside of the company. Whereas it had been viewed as a group of the cool kids on campus at the original device's announcement, eight months later, few wanted to be associated with the hardware or with Windows 8.

Though everyone knew that a Surface RT 2 would follow a similar path as the original device, Microsoft pushed forward. Panay and his team hoped that by the time they reached a third-generation device, they would be on the right path to success. Surface RT 2 would only buy them time, it was a stop-gap until they could get the formula right.

The development of the original Surface RT and Surface Pro were kept secret, but with those products now far behind Microsoft, development of the next generation became sloppy by comparison.

Even though the second generation of devices was released a year after the first, they had been in development for nearly 18 months by that point. Around the time that Microsoft had shown off the first generation Surface devices, the company began working on the next generation hardware. So, by the time Surface RT and Surface Pro were released, Microsoft was six months deep into development of the next generation devices.

Ahead of the Surface RT 2 /Pro 2 announcements, nearly all of the product details had leaked. Here's how it happened.

At this point in my writing career, back in 2013, I was starting to get traction and some recognition for my work; something that takes years in an industry where anyone can start a blog.

Luckily for me, this time, Microsoft wasn't doing a great job at keeping its upcoming hardware behind closed doors. Someone had taken a Surface prototype out of the labs and was using it in the Commons at Microsoft's Redmond campus. An insider, whose identity I still don't know to this day, sent me an email with images of the new hardware attached. But there was a catch. They asked that I not publish them.

The pictures confirmed that the device's kickstand would have two positions, instead of one like the original hardware. And some crudely-drawn schematics identified that the screen resolution was 1080p, or 1920 x 1080, a significant improvement over that of the original Surface RT.

But having this information and not being able to publish was a challenge. When publishing insider information, I always try to have two independent sources to verify the content. Once it's on the front page of any website, there is no way to go remove it from the pages of history.

But I took a risk. The photos proved that the device was real, so I published one of my first big scoops. Microsoft, I wrote, was building a second-generation Surface RT.

The post was deliberately vague, only noting that the device was coming in the near future and that it would have a modest specifications bump. But this accomplished my goal, it got me on Microsoft's radar. And the firm quickly reached out, wanting to know what other information I had; this also started me down a path that would lead to bigger and better things.

Soon after publishing this post, I contacted ZDNet's Mary Jo Foley about the information that I had but could not publish. I was looking for a second source to confirm the information. And I was afraid that what I had published might lead back to the person who sent it to me. Mary Jo told me I needed to contact Paul Thurrott. Since I barely knew him at the time and wasn't quite ready to reach out; I ignored her advice.

About a week later, Mary Jo asked me via Skype if I had reached out to Paul. I told her I had not, stating that I didn't know him all that well or even have his Skype contact information. Thirty seconds later, she added Paul to the chat and in all caps stated that the three of us combined had all the information for Surface RT 2 and needed to figure out how we were going to post it all.

At this time, Paul had received a PowerPoint presentation describing the new hardware but was in a similar situation to me: He knew what was coming but could not post it publicly. Paul and I shared notes, not realizing that this would be the start of a friendship that would eventually lead to us working together several years later.

One crucial detail I learned about the hardware was that it was not black even though the images I had seen of the early device had the same color as the original device. Instead, the new hardware was silver, the natural color of the magnesium with which it was made. As it turns out, many purchasers of the original devices complained that the black paint scratched too easily.

Thankfully I never published this detail, as it led Microsoft and its PR company down a separate path when trying to uncover the source of information. Both Microsoft and its PR company assumed that Paul and I had the slide deck when I did not.

I learned many years later that this leak made them realize that Surface development needed to happen in isolation away from others at the company and that they needed better protocols about how to handle sensitive information relating to hardware. Paul was later told the same by Panay, who seemed to think there was an internal conspiracy to sink Surface.

While much of the attention focused on the Surface RT 2, information about Surface Pro 2 was also mixed in with this information. But for outsiders like myself and many others, Surface RT 2 is what is always remembered because that was the device with which Microsoft was trying to change the ecosystem.

A new kind of PC with an ARM-based chipset was far more exciting than yet another Intel-based PC. After all, Intel was the established market leader in microprocessors. If Microsoft could have successfully sold tablets with ARM-based chipsets, the market today would likely look a lot different. But instead, Intel still dominates the market.

Indeed, Microsoft is once again trying to push the market towards ARM-based PCs as I write this, which shows how important this need still is. They are once again trying to win where the RT devices failed but with a new generation of hardware.

From late August to early September of that year, Paul and I leaked nearly every detail about the hardware and accessories that would be released. But even with all the information out in the wild, there were still subtle nuances to the release of the second generation of devices that would not be revealed until years later.

Chapter 9 - Second Generation RT and Pro

"We did what we had to do, we couldn't back down - yet."

In late September 2013, Microsoft announced the second generation Surface Pro and RT tablet PCs. But this event was quite different from the previous launch. The atmosphere was calmer, the hysteria over creating a new business organization had died down, and the devices were presented in a more "modern" fashion; this time, it was only Panay on the stage.

When Panay walked out on to the stage, he used a new DJ Type Cover that he said the company would eventually sell to turn down the music at the event. That device was never sold, though the company continued to promise that the Surface Cover port would be used to expand the functionality of the device. But their efforts always came up short and besides typing covers, nothing substantial ever materialized.

During this event, Panay's methodical preparation was discussed publicly, a rarity; he noted that the keynote length was about 4,000 steps. The presentation itself was about forty minutes long, but steps are important to Panay as they mean he is part of a "living" presentation. If he is static, he believes, so is the keynote. And that's why he likes to move around the stage and keep track of his steps to each station on the stage.

This time, Panay kicked off with the Surface Pro 2, instead of Surface 2, the second-generation RT device. This was intentional. The team knew that one of the devices they were announcing would sell and that the other would be another lackluster showing.

Choosing his words carefully, Panay noted that the original Surface

Pro was the best-selling device in its class. At face value, this sounds impressive for a new piece of hardware that was poorly launched and utilized one of Microsoft's biggest mistakes as its OS. But a bit of digging revealed that this was not as impressive as first appeared.

At the time of the original Pro's announcement, the market for "professional tablets" was not well-established. Other companies had yet to truly respond to Microsoft's call for touch-first PCs and the Surface Pro stood alone. It was even mocked by competitors. So while Surface Pro was indeed the best-selling the device in its category, it was also almost in a class by itself. Its only serious challenger was Apple's iPad, and that was absolutely not the same class of device.

With Surface Pro 2, Microsoft refined the formula, giving it a faster processor, better graphics, and updated display and audio. but the biggest change was to the kickstand. Where the original Surface Pro kickstand opened to only one position, the version in Pro 2 now had two locking stops. This, again, was a step on the path to where the team wanted to take the device with a universal position kickstand. But the technology wasn't fully ready and so the decision was made to go with the two stop design.

While demonstrating the new kickstand, Panay targeted some of the strongest criticism of the original Pro; it didn't work well on your lap. "Lappability," a term invented because of Surface, is the ability to use the hardware on your lap, like a traditional laptop. The original Pro, because of the angle of the kickstand and its top-heavy design, came up short in this scenario; it was unstable on your legs.

Surface Pro 2 and Surface 2 looked to remedy this problem. But the updated kickstand didn't address the device's high center of gravity. Even though Microsoft had hoped that this would fix the issue, the Surface team would later say that they had not done enough, and the lappability problem is a legacy that still comes up in nearly every Surface review.

But the real elephant in the room with Surface was battery life.

It was like a Ferrari that could drive only six miles on a tank of gas. The company did a good job of making the original Surface Pro incredibly fast, but it had sacrificed battery life. So it sought to solve this issue with the second generation via a two-pronged approach involving larger batteries and more batteries.

When designing the Surface Pro 2, it was possible to cram higher capacity batteries into the shell of the device but there were challenges that had to be overcome. More batteries meant more weight and this is a tricky balance because, with a device that has a high center of gravity, more weight means it will not sit a well on your lap and it becomes harder to hold for longer durations.

But the company knew that it had to extend the battery life and hoped that the new kickstand position would make the device more lappable. With a longer battery life, the ultimate laptop, tablet, and desktop (with the dock accessory) would sell better than the first generation.

Panay and his team were able to extend the battery life by several hours with the new generation without compromising on the original design but it was still far from perfect. While Surface Pro 2 was moving in the direction that was needed to help sell more units, it was still the awkward duck in the market as consumers had not warmed up to the idea of a powerful Windows tablet. It was missing a critical differentiator from other laptops and tablets.

Microsoft wanted the Surface Pro line to be a one-stop-shop for everything which is why we saw the company go all-in with a variety of accessories. But in its attempt to make a device that was a jack of all trades, it sacrificed on one key metric, mastering any of them.

With the safe(er) bet out of the way, the Surface 2 was introduced as a revamp of the original device. With an improved screen that supported a higher resolution, faster memory, CPU, and overall, a spec bump in nearly every category, the second generation Surface RT was neither a gamble nor aspiration, but a stepping stone to see if a market could be created in a world dominated by Intel.

But no matter how good the hardware, it was still running Windows RT, or in this case, Windows RT 8.1.

And this was the issue. Panay and his team were building new hardware that was running on possibly the worst version of Windows ever created. The store had no apps and the OS was confusing, but the hardware was magnificent by most accounts. But that didn't matter. The hardware that was supposed to get out of the way only emphasized the shortcomings of the OS, and this would force Surface 2 down the same path as Surface RT.

Even with the shortcomings of the operating system, there were inklings of serious change happening inside of the Surface team. They were beginning to understand that Surface needed a differentiator, something that others were not doing.

The company had tried to do this by including a free copy of Microsoft Office with Surface 2, adding enhanced functionality with SkyDrive (later renamed to OneDrive) and creating a unique set of accessories. But this wasn't enough.

We know now that Surface 2 was another failure for the company because it never built a Windows RT-based Surface 3. While the company took a significantly more cautious approach and restricted the number of units it ordered to avoid a write-down, the product failed to gain any momentum in the market.

And the Surface 2 failure surprised exactly no one. Microsoft insiders knew before the launch of this hardware that it would fail. And the company was already making preparations for the third-generation of devices that would eventually not include an RT branded device; this happened before the release of the second generation hardware.

One interesting thing that Microsoft did do with the second generation devices was to replace the Microsoft branding on the back of the device with the Surface name. When showing this change at the launch, Panay pitched it as the company wanting to promote the brand. But the reality was that Microsoft's corporate leadership didn't want the second generation Surface to sink the mothership if it went down in flames like the first generation.

Having learned from the earlier write-down, Microsoft was in a better position to determine the price for both devices in the market. Unlike launching the first generation hardware, the company had hard market data to better understand where the tipping point was for the consumer.

Early rumors suggested that Microsoft would not drop the entry-level price for the second generation hardware, meaning it would retain the same $499 price point. But Microsoft knew that this was not going to work. And in the final hours, it decided to cut its margin and ship Surface 2 starting at $449 instead; Surface Pro would start at $899.

To help bolster the perceived value of Surface 2, Microsoft sweetened the deal by adding free Skype calling and 200 GB of the company's SkyDrive cloud storage platform in addition to Office. For Surface Pro 2, Microsoft only included the Skype and SkyDrive add-ons because it believed that Office for professionals should still be purchased. The company also knew at that time that Surface Pro 2 would sell significantly better than the Surface 2, so including Office was less of a risk.

But even before it launched, there were whispers inside of the Microsoft offices that another RT device, no matter how good the hardware, would be a black eye for the company. Insiders, especially those near the top of the org chart, knew that this would be the last of the RT generation.

Chapter 10 - The Accessories of Hope

"We needed an ecosystem, even if it was an ecosystem of us"

One of the reasons that Apple's iPhones and iPads are so incredibly popular is that there is an accessory for everything. If you want to be a photographer or a musician, you can find a peripheral that pairs with the hardware to achieve that goal. The Surface team dreamed of having the same breadth of accessory offerings for Surface. But after a failed hardware release, it's a bit harder to convince other companies to make a strategic bet on your product.

To accomplish its goal of a thriving ecosystem of products, the company took this mission into its own hands. Granted, Microsoft was forced to do so as few third-party firms were willing to invest in Surface accessories in any serious capacity aside from cases. But it also helped that Microsoft understood the abilities of the port on the bottom of the device—now called the Surface Type Cover port—better than outside companies.

During the announcement of the second generation devices, Panay slowly introduced a new line of accessories. The goal was to expand the versatility of the PCs and show that Surface was becoming a real product line with a real ecosystem that would help customers personalize their experiences.

Even though the first generation hardware was by nearly all measurements a failure, there were glimmering lights of hope. The innovative Type Cover, which combined a protective cover with a real keyboard and trackpad, had resonated well with customers. The Touch Cover, which was similar but featured a flat, glass-like keyboard, meanwhile, was far less well-received; this actually surprised a few at the company who believed this keyboard cover would be a best-seller.

At this point in the tech industry, thin was in. Apple was shaving millimeters off of every device release and Microsoft didn't want to be left out of the race to make the thinnest devices imaginable. The Touch Cover was a unique way of inputting text that offered a bit more tactile feedback than typing on glass, while saving screen space since a virtual keyboard was not needed. And Microsoft hoped that it would eventually be the preferred way that users would type on the Surface.

With the second generation of the Touch Cover, Microsoft created a "blade," as they called it, that had over 1,000 sensors, significantly more than the 86 in the original cover. With this many sensors, input would be more accurate, gestures could be supported, and, crucially, it could be modified in many ways by simply changing the layout on the top piece of felt.

Surface 2 Touch Cover

The team that created this blade had lofty ambitions as well. The company hoped that by creating a blank canvas with the blade and a bunch of sensors, that it would spawn different iterations of the Touch Cover that could enhance the device. Everything from an art pallet to a game controller was envisioned, and some were even prototyped. But only one was ever shown to the outside world, the Music Kit.

When Panay walked out on stage during the Surface 2/Pro 2 announcement, he used the Music Kit to turn down the volume and later demoed the product, highlighting how it unlocked the creativity of the Surface platform. But there was one little problem, Microsoft would never sell the device.

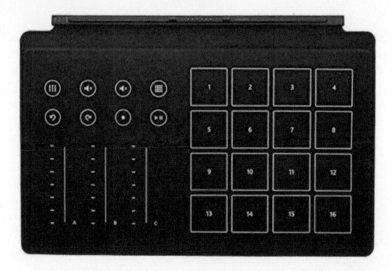

Surface Music Kit

During the life of the Surface brand, the company has canceled products but rarely have they announced a device/peripheral and then not widely distribute it. But the Music Kit is an exception, an example of the Surface team promising a product and not delivering it.

The problem was that the Music Kit involved too many groups inside the company and internal collaboration, which, at this time was more of a barrier than a high point for the organization. To make the Music Kit a reality, the Surface Team needed to build the product, the Windows team needed to enable the functionality in Windows, and then a team needed to build the actual software the Music Kit would use to create music.

Microsoft did put forth a notable effort to build this accessory but as time progressed, the pieces were not fitting together fast enough. The latency between the blade and the software was too large for actual DJs to mix music in real-time. And the functionality was too limited for it to be considered a serious alternative to professional DJ equipment.

In the end, the product was headed down a road of being too niche and the experience wasn't good enough for it to be offered to consumers. And there was always the uncertainty of releasing a product that would not be a success. The wounds of the past inventory adjustment had everyone at Microsoft back on their heels. And the idea of taking a risk to show what the Surface could do in an era of when the brand was teetering on imploding didn't make much financial sense.

Looking back at how the Surface brand has evolved, thinking that it was anything other than a productivity-focused device seems absurd. But that's the case and while the company announced a docking station called Surface Dock at the Surface 2/Pro 2 event, it was only at the last minute that the product was even created.

Surface Dock

When developing the accessories for the launch of the second generation of hardware, Microsoft was still focused on shipping a consumer product as it was still holding out that Windows RT would take off and become its OS of the future. But this was just tunnel vision, and the firm was ignoring its most profitable business segments and most loyal customers.

The Surface 2/Pro 2 roadmaps initially did not include a dock. Employees who insisted that the company should create one were agitated by this as they felt that the Pro was the beacon of light in the Surface brand and it was being underserved. To get around this, employees discussed approaching Belkin and Logitech to create a Surface dock so that it would be easier to sell their own product to corporate customers.

When the Surface team caught wind of this, Ralf Groene and his team created a prototype of their own dock in one day; within four hours of starting on the project, they had a prototype. While it was previously argued that the team didn't have enough resources to ship this product with the release of the Pro 2, his team was able to pull a few strings and get the product ready for release in short order.

It was a good decision. The Surface Pro Dock had a roughly 50% attachment rate in the corporate market, meaning, that 1 of every 2 Surface Pro purchases for the corporate market also included a dock. Not too bad for a peripheral the company almost didn't create.

Type Cover with BlueTooth adapter

Microsoft had such high confidence in its Type Covers that it thought people may want to use them when not connected to a Surface. So it created a BlueTooth adapter that was powered by an internal battery and let customer use an existing Type Cover wirelessly; the company did make this product available for sale, but only briefly.

Power Cover was another accessory that made a lot of sense, though the company has unfortunately never made the second iteration. This useful hybrid peripheral worked like a normal Type Cover but it also solved one of the primary complaints of the early Surface devices: Battery life was often significantly less when compared to other PCs of the day. The Power Cover was a thicker Type Cover with a battery under the keyboard.

Surface Power Cover

The accessory roughly doubled the life of the tablet, and it helped with the top-heavy problem, too. At a cost of $199.99, it wasn't cheap. But for those who needed maximum battery life, this was a worthwhile investment, albeit only for that one generation of Surface PCs.

For Microsoft, the keyboard covers have proven to be an excellent accessory for the Surface brand, and they have a 95 percent attach rate. The company does not include the Touch/Type Covers in the box and this has proven to be a lucrative decision for the bottom line.

Microsoft initially promised that it would license the technology to connect to the port on the bottom of the Surface. But with such a high attachment rate for its own Type Covers, there were fears that letting third parties create their own keyboard covers would be problematic.

After all, if Microsoft lets companies like Logitech build keyboard covers, wouldn't this cannibalize their own sales? This would be especially true if some of these firms created superior products. So while the company could charge a royalty for access to the port, doing so would be far less lucrative than selling its own Type Covers.

Regardless, Microsoft knew that fancy keyboards would not make Surface a hit with consumers or the corporate world. Dramatic changes would be needed because the current path to success wasn't working at a rate that Microsoft's board would support.

Surface was becoming a distraction inside of Microsoft. The Windows software was in serious need of a reboot after the disastrous launch of Windows 8, Microsoft was in the process of acquiring the mobile assets from Nokia, and the core business of the company was under attack from all sides. All this made launching a new hardware product, especially one that alienated its partners, all the harder.

But Panay always wanted to build three Surface iterations. And he was convinced, that despite the adversity inside the company at

this time, his team had found a winning formula and was willing
to bet it all to get the product out the door.

Chapter 11 - Accidentally NFL

"We knew they would be called iPads, it was only a matter of time"

In May 2013, Microsoft and the National Football League (NFL) announced a new partnership that would bring the Redmond-based company's products into the limelight. The NFL's reach in viewership and influence among its fans cannot be understated and with a deal valued around $400 million, Microsoft was making a serious investment to bring a unique viewing experience to the Xbox One.

While the partnership between Microsoft and the NFL resulted in Surface tablets on the sidelines of every game and on TV during the pre-game shows, that's now how it was originally envisioned. Indeed, the addition of Surface hardware was an afterthought and almost wasn't included in the deal.

The NFL, like most business, is always looking for new business models and partners to help increase its revenues. With tablets becoming more popular, the league sketched up a new sponsorship opportunity and approached Microsoft about the idea. This started a long series of negotiations internally and with the league.

Initially, Windows marketing chief Tami Reller was approached, but she was not interested in working with the league. But the NFL's offer was pushed around internally and eventually, it ended up on the desk of Yusuf Mehdi, who was then in charge of Xbox product marketing.

The NFL envisioned a deal with Microsoft around tablets. But the timing was right for another Microsoft hardware product that would launch later that year, the Xbox One.

At the time, Microsoft's Xbox hardware was being repositioned as a home entertainment device for the living room. Microsoft wanted to bring the power of the PC to the living room and it was positioning the Xbox One to be that product.

In what can only be described as a gross misunderstanding of its Xbox user base, Microsoft designed the Xbox One to focus on entertainment first and then gaming. The company was hoping to make the device appeal to more customers and give the company a leg-up against other entrants in the growing market for the living-room digital entertainment market. But Microsoft missed the mark, again.

The problem is that gamers want the best possible gaming machine, and nothing more. And while Microsoft was focusing on building out other services and features, Sony was locking up better exclusive game titles for its upcoming PlayStation 4 video game console. As a result, Microsoft quickly fell behind Sony in sales by a margin of 2-to-1 when the two products were launched nearly simultaneously in late 2013. It had competed neck-to-neck with Sony in the previous generation of consoles, so falling behind this badly was a serious blow to the Xbox brand and to Microsoft.

This failure to understand the market significantly undercut the company's ability to turn the device announcement momentum into sales.

But during the Xbox One's development, Microsoft was able to work a deal with the NFL to create a unique viewing experience for those who watched football games on their consoles. The hope was that by offering the best experience to watch NFL games, Microsoft could sell more Xbox consoles. That dream never materialized, but its failure provided a boost to Surface.

At the time the NFL deal was announced, the use of Surface tablets by the NFL was secondary to the Xbox arrangement. It's likely that if the Xbox deal had never been worked-out, Surface never would have been part of the NFL viewing experience.

And there were serious challenges that had to be overcome for the tablets to make their way to the sidelines. The NFL couldn't simply say "yes, coaches and players will use this tablet." The tablets had to be approved by the coaches and competition committee before the hardware could be delivered to each team. But there was also another issue, the software had to be created as well.

Building software that would actually add value to coaches and players on the NFL sidelines is not a trivial task. The tried-and-true method of using paper printouts had in place for decades and was a well-oiled process. Introducing tablets that needed to be charged and required a significant amount of input to find the needed content was not an easy transition or pitch.

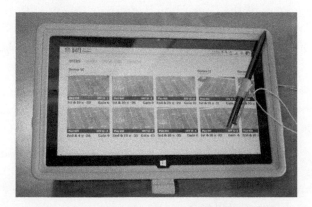

Surface NFL Tablet in its protective case

But in the end, Microsoft and the NFL were able to get the tablets to the sidelines of the NFL in what has become the best marketing aspect for the brand. The only issue was that the company and everyone on the marketing team knew that it was inevitable that the tablets would be called iPads or would be criticized by coaches and players.

Not only was the iPad the household name at that time, but Microsoft was injecting technology into a routine that was historically analog. Adjustment periods were common in the IT world but on the sidelines of a fast-moving professional sports game, there is a significantly smaller margin for error.

And it didn't take long for the first major PR disaster to occur. As expected, announcers frequently called the tablets "iPads," and every time they did so, the media would swarm on the screw-up and immediately question if Microsoft's $400 million deal was doing anything positive for the company or the Surface brand.

In the marketing playbook, trying to re-train the consumer to know a new brand when going up against a dominant player like Apple is a difficult challenge. But the challenges didn't stop with the misnaming. Coaches and players were starting to rebel as well.

Aaron Rodgers of the Green Bay Packers was spotted throwing a tablet. Worse for Microsoft was when the New England Patriots coach, Bill Belichick, ranted about the performance and consistency of the experience of using Surface on the sidelines.

In what became a famous animated GIF, Belichick slammed a tablet into the side of a Surface cart on the sideline after the device crashed while he was using it.

The early days of the tablets on the sideline created frequent fire drills for the marketing and support teams at Microsoft. But as the weeks and months went by, the number of flare-ups slowed down and momentum started to pick up.

One thing that may not have been apparent on the outside at the time is that the NFL deal may have saved Surface as a brand. At the time, Microsoft had just completed its acquisition of Nokia, and Steve Ballmer wanted to re-brand the company's hardware products. He felt that the previous baggage of write-downs had undermined the Surface brand, but the success of the NFL deal is one factor that attributed to Surface retaining its name.

Oddly, the NFL deal was not as big of a success for Xbox. For a product that was the "little brother" in the contract with the NFL, the Xbox had flatlined while Surface was on an upward trajectory.

The challenges that Surface faced in the early days of the NFL deal are far behind Microsoft at this point, and it has become a significant asset for the company. No longer is iPad the only name associated with tablets and with the software and hardware now significantly improved, Surface has proven to be an asset for NFL teams instead of a liability.

Chapter 12 - Eating Two Careers

"Nobody knows what HR does, but we all know a phone call from them is not good"

The turmoil in the early days of Surface was a turning point for Microsoft. The company, which was facing new competition as it had never seen in the prior two decades, needed to evolve. And that meant taking calculated risks.

Microsoft made billions in the enterprise with its productivity software. But it had always struggled in transitioning that success to consumers; Microsoft desperately wanted to be a company that consumers loved.

You can't fault it for a lack of effort either. Microsoft created consumer products like Windows Media Center, Zune, Microsoft Band, and Windows Phone. And it made an almost uncountable number of computer keyboards and mice over the decades. But all of that all faded into the background of the company's overall efforts; none were runaway hits, aside from the Xbox.

And even the Xbox, the company's best connection point with the consumer, has struggled. Especially after Microsoft completely misread the market with the launch of the Xbox One.

Steven Sinofsky is often remembered for the Windows 8 disaster. But to his credit, he had also come to Windows in the wake of the abysmal Windows Vista launch and he had to turn around the org; the company needed to make sure that Windows had a future.

At that time, Apple was full-throttle down the runway and moments away from takeoff; bolstered by the success of the iPod, the first modern company to hit a one trillion dollar valuation was coming for Microsoft.

With the now-famous "I'm a Mac and I'm a PC" series of commercials, Apple successfully swayed the market against Windows; Microsoft needed a fix.

Windows Vista was supposed to bring Windows into a new era of computing by modernizing the legacy infrastructure. And the company made promises that the operating system could never live up to, resulting in a reboot of the development process and long release delays. When the OS did launch, drivers and software were not ready which resulted in a poor user experience, with poor performance, frequent crashing, and loss of data.

Windows 7 was designed to fix these problems.

Sinofsky created a policy that Microsoft would not make any promises about what the OS would deliver to avoid the types of problems that sunk Vista. Until the team was certain a feature would ship with the release, it would not be discussed publicly.

This change in communication was a significant shift in how the company had previously built its operating systems. Because Microsoft depended on its partners to help sell Windows, the company would frequently and publicly disclose its development plans to make sure that the market would be ready for what was coming down the pipeline. After this type of development failed spectacularly with Vista, Windows 7 development marched to a much quieter beat, one that ultimately proved successful.

Even today, Windows 7 is often referred to as the best version of Windows ever created. And for Microsoft, it was a monumental success. The OS helped push its revenue needle higher and despite a few early compatibility hiccups, the operating system was rock solid; it is still the preferred choice for the corporate world to this day.

But the problem with Windows 7 was that it was not a touch-focused operating system. Microsoft and the entire world saw how a "touch-first" computing experience was revolutionizing mobile and it decided to build on the success of Windows 7 by taking a risk with Windows 8.

Sinofsky and his team doubled-down on the secrecy and followed up Windows 7 with Windows 8, a release that many regard as the biggest failure in the history of Windows. While Windows Vista certainly had its problems, it didn't disrupt the company's operating model. Windows 8 threatened to do just that.

A confusing failure for both consumers and businesses, Windows 8 changed Microsoft's future from a blue-sky world to a gray and dismal outlook. Ultimately, Steven Sinofsky would leave Microsoft as a result of this misstep. And while Microsoft and Sinofsky have never said explicitly why the two parted ways, he was asked to leave. And there are several factors that played into his career coming to an end at the company.

Most obviously, Windows 8 was a failure on nearly every front. From a sales perspective, it came up short compared to previous versions, and it failed to establish two other key areas Sinofksy had touted, touch input and a store for applications.

Many have linked the failure of the first generation of Surface PCs to the departure of Sinofsky. That may have had some impact on the decision, but Surface was always isolated financially from the revenue-producing parts of the company. In short, Surface could have failed by itself and not sunk the ship.

But with Windows failing too, and more importantly, PC makers suffering as well, Sinofsky had to go.

And it wasn't just the business performance. Sinofsky had been fighting for more control and had created walls inside the company that was fracturing its ability to compete cohesively. The timing was also right as well.

Before the official announcement came, there were early signs of a pending reorganization inside of Microsoft. At the company's developer conference, Build, Sinofsky did not present Windows 8, Instead, it was CEO Steve Ballmer who demonstrated the operating system.

Sinofsky's departure was finally announced by Ballmer on November 12, 2012. In a face-saving statement, both Microsoft and Sinofsky stated that Sinofksy decided to leave of his own accord. In his letter to employees, Sinofsky stated, "some might notice a bit of chatter speculating about this decision or timing. I can assure you that none could be true as this was a personal and private choice that in no way reflects any speculation or theories one might read— about me, opportunity, the company or its leadership.".

Some insiders at the company believe that Sinofsky was not fired. Instead, the two agreed that the timing was right and that because of the failure of two major products, his control over future decisions was in jeopardy. And with Windows 8 development completed, it was the natural time to make a change.

Ultimately, most agree that Sinofsky's departure came down to internal politics. Microsoft was failing to collaborate internally and Sinofsky was seen as the reason this was happening.

At the time, Sinofsky's departure was seen as an enormous shakeup. But there was an even bigger shakeup to come: Steve Ballmer would soon be leaving the company as well.

Ballmer had led Microsoft for 14 years by that point. And while his legacy is often tarnished by decisions late in his tenure, he does deserve credit for also reshaping Microsoft during a volatile time in history.

When he took over in January 2000, at the end of that fiscal year, Microsoft had annual revenues of $22.96 billion. When he left in early 2014, the company posted annual revenues of $86.8 billion. Any way you look at it, that is a significant increase for the company. But one metric that Ballmer was never able to overcome was the stock price. He had a finicky relationship with Wall Street, and Microsoft's share price typically wallowed in the $25 to $35 range during his entire tenure. No matter how much revenue the company delivered, its share price remained stagnant.

Unlike Sinofsky, Steve Ballmer was not fired from Microsoft. But the board helped push him in that direction after heavily criticizing his slow pace at turning things around following the Windows 8 launch. While the Surface write-down wasn't exactly a career high point, it was not the cause for his departure either.

Ultimately, Ballmer's decision to leave the company was his own. Coming to the self-realization that Microsoft would be better without him is the hallmark of a true leader. And Ballmer concluded just that, so he got the ball rolling himself.

In July 2013, Microsoft announced what may be one of the largest reorganizations in its history. And while the world at that time did not know that Ballmer would soon step down, this change was his final shakeup at the company. At least his final planned shake-up.

A month later, Steve Ballmer said that he would retire from Microsoft within one year. Following this announcement, the software giant began searching for candidates to replace him.

But Ballmer had one major change to implement before he exited the company. In September 2013, he announced that Microsoft would acquire Nokia's mobile phone assets for over $7 billion dollars in a last ditch effort to save its smartphone operating system, Windows Phone.

This acquisition *did* play a role in Ballmer's departure, as he wanted to buy Nokia in its entirety, specifically citing the company's mapping assets as a huge advantage for Microsoft. But the board of directors didn't want to purchase any part of Nokia let alone the entire company. And the board meeting at which Microsoft finally decided to pursue the Nokia acquisition was marked by a lot of shouting and high tension.

At that time, only Nokia, with its Lumia line of smartphones, was making a serious effort to help Microsoft claw back mobile market share. But those efforts started failing. Nokia shifted priorities and even released a line of phones based on Android. So Ballmer felt that Microsoft had to buy the Nokia assets to keep the Windows Phone dream alive. Otherwise, it would have to abandon the platform.

Microsoft eventually wrote-off the Nokia purchase after Ballmer's departure. And it exited the smartphone market anyway, losing more than $10 billion along the way.

But as Ballmer was preparing to leave the company, the Nokia assets had been purchased, and Windows was being shaken up with new leadership. And Panay and his team were quietly working away on the next iteration of Surface.

With so much turmoil happening inside the company, Surface's only hope at survival was a home run. And while no one said it publicly, if the next iteration of Surface failed to win in the market, the brand and the hardware would cease to exist.

Chapter 13 - The Future Depends on This

"He came for the name, thankfully he didn't win that fight"

Following the release of Surface 2 and Surface Pro 2, the team had one objective. It needed a hit product the world would love. Of course, this had been the goal all along, but it was now or never.

The second-generation Surface hardware followed a similar trajectory to the first iteration; Surface Pro 2 sold better than the RT-based Surface 2. But at least this time around, the company didn't have millions of units sitting in storage that needed to be accounted for financially. And this was what was expected; the second iteration would not be the device that would turn the brand around.

There was a lot of change happening at Microsoft at this time that raised the stakes even further. Steve Ballmer was looking to move beyond Microsoft by retiring as CEO, the entire company was accepting that Windows 8 was a flop, Windows RT was not turning out to be the future of the Windows platform, and Microsoft's smartphone bets were coming up short. So Surface sat on an island by itself as a product that needed a win to survive. But failure was looking like the future of that platform, too.

Everyone at Microsoft knew that if the upcoming release of the third generation Surface Pro was not a huge success, the leadership team would kill Surface. The investments, up to this point, had not delivered the returns needed to justify the product's existence. And the bigger issue of Microsoft alienating its PC maker partners was also making it tougher to justify the company being in the hardware space.

But from the beginning, Panay wanted three generations of Surface

PCs. And Microsoft was going to live up to its promise to let him build another iteration of the hardware.

The problem the team was facing was that in order to make Surface Pro 3 a success, they needed to make big changes to the hardware. But the sting of the earlier write-down was still fresh in everyone's minds and taking another large bet on hardware meant asking for more money.

Why not use readily available off-the-shelf components to build something unique and save a bit on the hardware while increasing margins on the hardware? That's the argument and it's tough to push back against that idea when the Surface brand wasn't a hit, and wasn't even well-known with really anyone at this point in time. And besides, the entire company was being overhauled with new leadership from the Windows organization to the CEO position. Would you want to make a huge bet on a product that had already failed to meet expectations twice before?

But that's exactly what Panay and his team did. They went all-in on Surface Pro 3 in an attempt to move the needle in a highly competitive PC market.

It wasn't until the third generation of Surface that Microsoft finally realized how their product could fit into the marketplace. While the Surface 2 series of devices started to show the new direction, it wasn't until Surface Pro 3 that Microsoft finally embraced its true strength, productivity.

Up until this point, Microsoft wanted the Surface brand to be everything Windows could be. But that was weighing down the product. Looking back, this was also about the time that Microsoft finally embraced that the company would not be a consumer-focused brand but one that enabled individuals and corporations to achieve more by using its products and services.

This wasn't an easy realization for the company. Even though survey after survey showed how and why people were buying

Surface hardware, the company wanted desperately to replicate Apple's entire success, but inside its own digital ecosystem.

The company had music services, a fitness wearable, mobile phones, and much more. But at the end of the day, Microsoft was a productivity company. And until it came to this realization, its previous efforts were a distraction from the primary course of growth.

And there was another challenge internally. Steve Ballmer didn't think that the Surface name was valued anymore and he felt that the company should abandon it. His suggestion was to rename the Surface devices to Win, using WinTab for the Surface Pro and WinBook for the Surface Book which was then in the early stages of development.

Panay and his team never took this suggestion seriously and continued building up the Surface brand. But this wouldn't be the last time that Ballmer tried to rename the hardware.

With its new productivity focus in mind, the company changed the tagline of the product. At this time, it was "the tablet that can replace your laptop." Ultimately, the idea that this tablet could replace a laptop was controversial, but the path was clear: Surface was a tablet that put productivity first.

This change in focus was subtly different than making one device designed to be equally good at consumption and creation. But by making the best productivity-focused tablet, one that could also replace a laptop, the device had a new clarity of purpose.

From a design perspective, the big bet that Microsoft made with Surface Pro 3 was to change the aspect ratio of the display from the typical widescreen 16:9 format to a squarer 3:2. In hindsight, this has become a key differentiator for all Surface PCs, a unique aspect ratio that fits better with the productivity theme than the entertainment aspect ratio of the earlier Surface products. Where 16:9 is ideal for watching movies, 3:2 is ideal for work.

Microsoft Office was one of the big drivers for this change. In a 16:9 arrangement, reading email on a Surface limited you to seeing only a few emails in Outlook. By switching to 3:2, you could now see more content on the display without sacrificing portability.

It may seem trivial, but this subtle but substantial change is what separated Surface Pro 3 from nearly every other product on the market. It was a huge gamble: if users didn't like the taller aspect ratio, then this device would be yet another flop for the company.

Critically, this change would also increase the cost of making the device. Even today, 16:9 is still the most popular aspect ratio for PC displays and nearly every production facility in the world is set up to create hardware with this layout. So producing a device with a new aspect ration would require retooling or lower production yields.

In simple terms, to produce a display with 3:2 aspect ratio, the glass used to create the displays would not be optimally cut and would result in excess glass that couldn't be used for a display. It's a substantial change, and with Microsoft in the midsts of a reorganization, it was a major request.

With this release, Microsoft would also start to push Surface to the company's most lucrative customer base for the first time, too; Microsoft would begin selling Surface Pro 3 in the corporate channel.

Today, this doesn't seem like a big consideration. But at the time, Microsoft was only offering its hardware products through con-sumer outlets like BestBuy, Staples, and its own retail and online stores. This left the business-focused channel to its partners like Dell, HP, Lenovo and many others. But Microsoft wanted to push Surface to those customers as well.

So the company began hiring and repositioning sales teams to get the product into the channel.

But there was a big hurdle. Terry Myerson, who now oversaw

Microsoft's Windows and hardware efforts, and Stephen Elop, who had come back to Microsoft with the Nokia acquisition, felt that Surface hardware should not be sold in the channel.

This was a decisive decision, one that was made to protect PC makers from Microsoft's own efforts to enter the PC market. But it came too late. The marketing team was already moving forward with this new direction and started building up the staff needed to execute the new strategy; a fight was brewing.

The final decision was escalated to the Senior Leadership Team. The SLT, as it is known internally, is where final decisions are made when business units do not agree about a strategic direction for the company.

The SLT determined that as long as Surface was positioned as a premium brand, it could argue to its PC partners that this hardware would help elevate the PC industry, not compete with it. Up until Surface launched, if an executive drove to work in a Ferrari wearing a $4000 suit and a $10,000 watch, the best thing he could pull out of his bag was the computing equivalent of a Toyota Camry. While companies like HP and Lenovo had some high-end machines, they mostly sold budget and mid-range PCs.

The premium PC space was open because few companies dared to compete head-to-head with Apple's line of MacBook Pro laptops; Apple commanded a premium price, something that Microsoft's partners could never achieve in volume with their own hardware. If Surface could fill that largely aspirational space, the SLT would buy-in.

The strategy worked. In the year following the release of Surface Pro 3, the corporate channel accounted for 50% of the sales of the device.

Positioning wasn't the only challenge: Microsoft finalized its acquisition of the Nokia assets during the later stages of development of the Pro 3, and Nokia's Lumia brand was part of those assets. At the time, the Lumia brand was far stronger than that of Surface, and that fact presented another opportunity to take a closer look at the Surface brand before its next major release.

The Lumia name is perfect in some ways. It's easily pronounced, short and concise, and easily recognizable, and it stood out better than the Surface brand. So Ballmer wanted to rename Surface Pro 3 to the Lumia Tab. There was just one problem: This decision came too late in the development cycle to change the hardware name because the marketing assets had already been created.

The only thing that saved Surface from being rebranded was the lengthy Nokia acquisition process. If Microsoft could have acquired the assets sooner, the Surface brand we know today would likely not exist.

The extended acquisition process also took its toll on Windows Phone. When Microsoft was performing its due diligence of Nokia, that firm's mobile devices organization had a robust lineup of devices that were being prepared for successive releases. But once Microsoft established that it would buy the assets, Nokia slashed research and development spending; the innovation pipeline at Nokia dried up overnight.

The acquisition was further delayed by a lengthy regulatory approval process from several countries, causing Nokia's reduced investment in new hardware to become depleted; Microsoft bought a Lumia brand whose future had been artificially cut short by its previous owners.

As a result, when Microsoft closed the deal, the new Lumia launches were all mid-grade, re-hashed handsets with subtly different display sizes rather than new hardware pushing boundaries like the innovative Lumia 1020. Microsoft was purchasing an empty shell.

Microsoft had to scramble to build the high-end phone that would eventually become the Lumia 950. But by the time it was finally ready for release, Microsoft's phone business had already collapsed.

And then there was Surface Mini.

In the run-up to the third-generation Surface, Panay and his team were working on two devices, Surface Pro 3 and a mini-tablet called Surface Mini. Ultimately, the company would only release the Surface Pro 3, but it was within minutes of shipping Surface Mini as well.

At the time, some at Microsoft believed that Windows on ARM could still be successful even though consumers were confused by the differences between Windows RT and "real" Windows.

Leading up to the Surface Pro 3 and Surface Mini launch event, I had written dozens of articles about Surface Mini. This included everything from how it was going to be different from the larger Surface Pro 3 to its expected availability; I had seen documents detailing the launch strategy for the device.

Even though Microsoft's leadership team was not sure whether the Mini was a good idea, Panay and his team kept pushing forward with the hardware and began producing early samples of the device; these early prototypes were distributed internally for testing.

The early feedback was that the hardware was exceptional for taking notes and that it was a better device for meetings than a laptop. But, management was unsure if this device would sell.

With its future uncertain, the launch date got closer, and the development of Surface Mini marketing materials commenced. Its market position was identified and the team kept working to make sure that if this product launched; all the parts were in place to give it the best shot at success.

During this timeframe there was another big change. Steve Ballmer officially stepped down as the CEO of Microsoft and Satya Nadella took over as the company's new leader.

Mr. Nadella became the new CEO on February 4, 2014, just three months before the next Surface launch event. And if that wasn't enough turbulence for the company, Microsoft closed on its acquisition of Nokia's mobile assets on April 25. And Stephen Elop was joining Microsoft and would lead the company's overall devices efforts.

With a new CEO and a new manager, everything hardware-related at Microsoft was undergoing new reviews, and strategic priorities would be changing. With Surface having not found success in any meaningful way to grow Microsoft's bottom-line, the tension leading up to the release of the next generation of hardware could not have been higher.

Panay and his team didn't need a good device, they needed a home run if they wanted to be around the following year.

Chapter 14 - Surface Pro 3 Debut

"The invites were already sent out, there was nothing we could do"

On May 4th, Microsoft sent out media invites for a hardware announcement that would take place in New York City. The tagline for the event was "Join us for a small gathering" which tipped off the media and everyone else that the company was preparing to release the long-rumored Surface Mini. Rumors also swirled that there would also be a larger device announced too.

In the weeks prior, Panay and his team were wrapping up the final details for the launch, including determining how the products would be positioned. Deciding Surface Mini or Surface Pro 3 would be showcased first mattered, but that decision would be made easier when Surface Mini was scrapped before launch.

Microsoft made the decision to not ship Surface Mini about 48 hours after the press invites went out. In a heated meeting, Panay defended the product and argued that the company needed to sell the hardware. But the decision was made by the leadership team to focus on the new Pro; the company was confident that this was the right product with the best chance of success.

Stephen Elop is often targeted as a key reason Surface Mini never made it to market. But the reality is that it was a group decision by Microsoft's SLT to not ship the hardware. Surface Mini, which ran Windows RT, came up short in many areas. But it was one area in particular that kept the device from reaching retail shelves.

Microsoft was in the process of pivoting the Surface brand from being an all-encompassing entertainment device to being productivity focused. The problem for the Surface Mini was that it wasn't going to be the most productive small tablet on the market. It was neutered by the version of Microsoft Office it was using, Office RT.

In March 2014, Satya Nadella made one of his first big decisions as CEO by pushing to release Office for the iPad ahead of the version for the Windows Store and Windows RT. And a few weeks prior to Microsoft sending out the invites to its hardware event, the company did just that

There was serious concern that if the iPad Mini were compared to the Surface Mini, Apple's tablet would beat Microsoft's device in the category it was trying to win, productivity.

But there were other reasons why the Surface Mini was canceled, too. The future of Windows RT was in jeopardy, as no vendors aside from Nokia made any serious bets on the OS and performance continued to lag significantly behind that of Intel. By removing Windows RT and Surface Mini from the equation, Microsoft could focus directly on the product that they knew would sell, Surface Pro 3.

Canceling Surface Mini this late in the development cycle presented a number of serious challenges. All of the marketing assets for the upcoming event had been produced and had to be reclaimed and restructured. And Panay would have to rework his presentation, a significant undertaking this late in the project.

By this time, Panay and his team had already been working to establish the presentation cadence. Eliminating 50% of the announcements presented serious challenges about how to extend the length of the stage-time to justify the launch event.

But the story of the Surface Mini does not stop there.

As Microsoft was working feverishly to claw back all the devices that had been distributed, one of them went missing; a junior staffer at Microsoft had "lost" a Surface Mini somewhere on campus.

While the removal of Surface Mini from the keynote was creating an unneeded distraction from the ongoing preparation work for Surface Pro 3, the clock was ticking and the keynote was quickly approaching.

Prior to the launch of Surface Pro 3, Microsoft wanted feedback about the changes they were going to make to the hardware. With the new aspect ratio and other features coming to the device, it began showing off the hardware prior to its announcement to channel partners and retailers for insight. The feedback was very positive.

In hindsight, this is when the company knew that the product they would soon announce was going to be a success. Surface Pro 3 was different but also the same, with its embrace of productivity, the new aspect ratio, the updated specs, and the new partner strategy, the hard work leading up to this point was finally starting to pay dividends.

With confidence growing, the Surface Mini canned, and the press invites sent out, Panay and his team were ready to show the world what they knew was going to be the hero device the company had longed desired.

At a studio in New York City—notable to the press in attendance

for having some of the worst seats ever for a Microsoft event—
Satya Nadella walked out on stage to kick things off. This was
an important moment for Microsoft and if the newly-minted CEO
hadn't shown up for the announcement, it may have undermined
the company's ambitions to build out the Surface brand. If the CEO
wasn't going to attend the event, why should anyone else care
about what the hardware team was doing?

When Satya invited Panay on stage, the two shared a brief hand-
shake and a hug. This was an important departure from the icy
interaction between Ballmer and Sinofsky at the first Surface event.
You could tell that there was a stronger bond between Panay and
Nadella than between Sinofsky and Ballmer.

Following Nadella, Panay began working the crowd, relaxing them
in the process, and preparing them for the next generation of
Surface.

He wasted no time as he began to drum up the theme of productivity and how he envisioned Surface as a device that would help its
users be more efficient at the tasks they were trying to accomplish.

Apple's iPad had been announced three years prior to Surface Pro
3, and it was supposed to make the laptop a thing of the past.
But at the Surface Pro 3 keynote, Panay joked about how hardly
anyone in the audience was using a tablet; left unsaid, however,
was that a significant majority of the assembled press were using
Apple MacBooks, not Windows laptops. It wasn't just that the iPad
that Apple hadn't caught on as a productivity device, Macs were
also becoming a serious threat to Microsoft's mission with Surface
as well.

But more importantly, Panay pointed out that based on market
research, 96% of people who own an iPad also own a laptop.

Panay was constructing a narrative for how Microsoft envisioned
that Surface Pro 3 would fit into the marketplace. With the iPad
unable to replace a laptop, the company was hoping that they had
a device that would beat Apple's hardware and catapult Surface

as a brand and product that combined the best of both tablet and laptop.

Pacing the stage, Panay made the argument that buying a tablet or a laptop came down to compromising on what you wanted to do with the device; consume or create? This was the choice that he said users were making when they walked into an Apple Store and that they could be conflicted about which device to buy.

After setting of the stage for what Surface Pro 3 aspired to be, Panay paused for a moment and with a determined and confident look on his face said "today we take the conflict away and I'm absolutely sure of that."

Pulling out a Surface Pro 3, he said, "this is the tablet that can replace your laptop." A bold claim, as Panay and his team had tried to accomplish this task with two previous iterations and had failed. But with their backs up against the wall, Surface Pro 3 was their pinnacle achievement: It was what Panay had set out to do, several years before.

The new hardware was thinner and faster, and the battery life was longer. But what Panay focused on is what finally made Surface different than everything else on the market at that time, its 12-inch 3:2 display.

Peppered into his description of the new hardware, the word productivity appeared again and again. He positioned this device as not "the best of Windows," as with previous Surface PCs, but as the "best of productivity." And he acknowledged this shift by adding, "productivity, not a sexy word, I totally get it."

But this newfound focus for the company was critically important for Microsoft as it gave the company a north star to chase. And Panay putting productivity front and center for Surface would eventually push others inside the company to recognize this was the correct focus for Microsoft. Its previous efforts to mask this were disingenuous to the company's mission and proved to be nothing more than a distraction.

During this event, Microsoft and Panay made it clear that they were targeting the premium brands of the world, specifically Apple. On stage, Panay demonstrated how the tablet weighed less than the MacBook Air. And its higher resolution display meant you could fit more content on-screen with Surface Pro 3 when compared to the MacBook Air.

This positioning also set the stage for how this device would be reviewed. Microsoft was setting a high bar; not only could Surface Pro 3 replace your laptop, but it could also replace one of the best laptops on the market at that time, the MacBook Air.

After showing the world why Surface Pro 3 could replace a tablet and a laptop, the keynote shifted even more deeply into productivity. There were demonstrations with a new Surface Dock and Microsoft showed how different applications for creative professionals would load instantaneously. More importantly, Microsoft had been working with Adobe to make the experience on the Surface Pro 3 better than the competition.

This was important for Microsoft as it showed that using the pen and touch wasn't strictly a novelty but that Surface Pro 3 enabled a unique way to interact with the upcoming version of Photoshop. That being said, the on-stage demo was a bit rough around the edges and not everyone was pleased with how Adobe presented themselves that day. The demo featured a few scribbles of the newly-christened Surface screen, gesture input that was far from smooth, and the demo only last about 65 seconds.

The challenge of lappability remained at the forefront of the Surface Pro 3 conversation. So Panay and his team introduced two new features that they hoped would finally solve the lapability riddle; a kickstand that worked in any position and a new magnetic strip on the Type cover that let users choose a more comfortable typing angle.

These changes did make a big difference in terms of lappability and overall stability. The Surface Pro series still suffers from being a top-heavy device, since the entire computer is in the display, but the updates to the Type Cover for this generation made a significant difference when using the device on your lap.

But there was something missing from the stage: The Touch Covers that the company had previously championed were no longer being offered. They were not loved by anyone who wasn't working on the product and consumer voted with their pocketbooks, the Type Cover was king.

The Touch Cover is a perfect example of something that makes sense on paper but not when produced. Despite their best effort to make this product a defining feature of the Surface brand, with the Surface Pro 3, the Touch Cover was dead.

Panay ended his presentation by telling the audience that they couldn't experience the difference until they felt the product in their own hands. With a confidence that this would be the hardware that would change the direction of the Surface brand forever, Microsoft handed out the tablet that day to press and analysts, something it doesn't do very often these days.

But there was something else missing from the event and it became obvious towards the end of the presentation. The event seemed to drag on, and it wasn't a typical finish. What the press didn't realize was that Panay had to fill time on stage: A 30-minute presentation to announce a single product would have been too short.

Microsoft's "small gathering" was only small in the number of products announced; the heavily-rumored Surface Mini was real, but it was gone forever.

Chapter 15 - The Lost Mini

"Of course you found the one that we could not"

When Microsoft decided to not ship the Surface Mini, it put into motion a series of events that the company had not experienced before. It had never canceled a hardware product this close to release.

Even though those who used the device internally love Surface Mini, it still suffered from the issues that doomed previous Surface PCs built on the ARM platform: Windows RT was a confusing mess and there was no high profile third-party software available. For a company that was trying to rescue the Surface brand, betting on Windows RT simply didn't make sense.

Granted, Windows 8 wasn't exactly a peach either. But it was the best available option for the Surface Pro 3 and as history now shows, it was this device that turned the tides for the brand.

But scrubbing Surface Mini was complex. There were banners, marketing material, and pamphlets that all had to be scrapped. Further, the company didn't want to acknowledge all the leaks around the device or even hint that the hardware was real or was ever coming to market.

Following the Surface Pro 3 launch event, some Microsoft employees had fun poking at the reporters who had written up leaks about the "mythical" Surface Mini. But for those of us who had written about Surface Mini, and knew it was real, the bigger concern was what had really happened. Were the Surface Mini stories leaked deliberately so that Microsoft could figure out who their sources were? That is always an issue, as is protecting those who provide the insights that help us do our reporting.

At that time, it was a bit confusing that the product wasn't announced, but more evidence that the hardware was real would soon show its face. With reviewers getting early access to Surface Pro 3, Microsoft the following day sent them a product guide with more information about the device. But the company forgot to proof it before signing off on the document, and it was filled with references to Surface Mini. Oops.

I later learned that the product guide had been finalized about 72 hours before the Surface Mini was canceled. Because of the close turnaround between scrubbing the marketing material and reviewing the product guide, the dates looked close enough that the sign-off appeared to cover the timeline of the canceling. Therefore, it didn't need to be re-reviewed.

Not long after the guide went out, numerous publications wrote about the un-released hardware. This was embarrassing for Microsoft but the firm was also concerned that this revelation would distract from the positive press wave that typically follows the announcement of a new device.

On September 22, I received a message from a source that said, "Do you want to see a Surface Mini?" The obvious answer to that question was "Yes." But I had to fly to Seattle to do so.

Not wanting to pass up the chance, I booked my flight to Seattle on the 23rd for a meeting on the 24th.

I don't know how much Microsoft pays attention to the journalists who cover the company, but had I broadcasted that I was on my way to Seattle, it would likely have set off a few alarms. So I remained silent and perhaps over-compensated for my secret travel by scheduling tweets and other posts to make it appear that I was doing anything other than getting on a plane headed to Seattle, Washington.

The person who I was meeting had found a Surface Mini sitting in a cabinet in an unoccupied location. I don't want to list the location, as the person still works for Microsoft. But, yes, this was the lost Surface Mini. This person had found it by accident and was willing to show it to me.

The Surface Mini had an 8-inch display, a Qualcomm Snapdragon 800 processor, 1 GB of RAM, USB support, and a microSD card reader, and it utilized a Surface Pen like Surface Pro 3. The outside of the device was a bit different from that of Pro 3. It would have come in different colors thanks to the case the company was also creating that fully covered the device.

Calling it a case may not be entirely accurate as it was built into the device. Though it felt like something that could be removed, it was attached to the device permanently.

The hardware would have been excellent for taking notes, but the slower processor and Windows RT 8.1 doomed it from ever reaching the market. The turmoil inside of Microsoft at that time made it too risky of a bet to launch the hardware but I do wonder if the company would reconsider this today with its renewed focus on making Windows on ARM a mainstream reality.

At about 5 pm that day, I tweeted out a picture from the center of Microsoft's campus, showing that I was there. Having played with the device and received the information that I needed to write a Surface Mini obituary, I wanted an official comment from Microsoft.

Popping up on campus like this will set off alarm bells. A few years later I learned that Microsoft marketing head Frank Shaw emailed the firm's PR company Waggener Edstrom, with a simple question, "Why is Brad here?" He was then informed about the information and pictures I had of the unreleased hardware.

The real question was what happened to the remaining Surface Mini tablets that had been produced? For the most part, they were destroyed. But a lucky few on campus still have the devices. While they have never shown the hardware to the public, I was eventually able to publish some of the pictures I obtained.

In the end, the decision to stick with Surface Pro 3 and to cancel Surface Mini made sense at the time. But the company knew it would eventually have to expand Surface beyond the tablet market and explore additional form-factors if its long-term ambitions to own the premium segment of the PC market would be successful.

Chapter 16 - Everyone is Mad at Microsoft

"They wouldn't always tell us, but we knew"

Onstage at the Surface Pro 3 launch, Nadella talked about the company's ambitions in the hardware space. He said, "We are not interested in competing with our [partners] when it comes to hardware." But there was only one problem with that statement: Microsoft *was* competing with its PC maker partners. And they were livid that Microsoft was entrenching themselves in the marketplace with Surface.

The PC industry is incredibly competitive with a wide range of companies making hardware including Dell, HP, Lenovo, Asus, Acer, Razer and many more. When Microsoft announced that it too would be entering the hardware space, they were highly upset with the software giant. Sometimes publicly. And often privately.

From the first iteration of Surface, Microsoft received strong feedback from these partners. Acer CEO JT Wang hit back first and criticized Microsoft publicly in August 2012 in an interview with the Financial Times.

"Think twice," he said to Microsoft openly in that interview. "It will create a huge negative impact for the ecosystem, and other brands may take a negative reaction. It is not something you are good at so please think twice." Not mincing words, he called out Microsoft for venturing into Acer's territory and for not being good at building hardware.

Not every company was publicly dismissing Microsoft's attempt at creating hardware. HP senior vice president John Solomon spoke to CRN, saying "our relationship has not changed at all due to

Microsoft's announcement. In fact, I applaud it — I think it's great that they are getting out in front and [showing] what's possible."

Regardless of what was being said publicly or privately, it was clear that Microsoft was upending the hardware space and changing the model for everyone. Even though the company worked closely with its partners, building both the software and the hardware gives the company a considerable advantage over its partners. There would always be a delay from OS release/update to making it available to hardware partners.

Behind closed doors, partners would speak more harshly about Microsoft to me when I was being briefed on new PC hardware. Especially during the first couple of generations, PC makers had no problem explicitly calling out Surface for its issues and Microsoft's immaturity in building PCs.

One PC maker in the fall of 2014 told me that Microsoft was bringing a knife to a gun fight when it came to building tablets. Another said that Microsoft's tablets would continue to fail because Microsoft would never be able to get the price low enough to sell in high volume.

To try and keep the peace with its partners, Microsoft started showing them pre-release Surface hardware to help them prepare for the upcoming launch. Microsoft says its goal was to never compete directly with its partners. That message was especially hard to convey in the early days of the product line and was often lost in the noise of the announcements.

But it's incredibly hard to launch a premium brand overnight. It takes years to achieve this status, and this was the message that was difficult to convey.

At the top end of the market, there was room for another player. Prior to the launch of the Surface brand, or more accurately, the Surface Pro 3, Apple had the top of the market to itself. Yes, other PC makers built high-end hardware, but they also built budget PCs too.

Microsoft wanted to compete only with Apple. And while PC makers were not on board with this idea at the beginning, as time passed, it became clear how Microsoft could co-exist with its partners. The Redmond-based company had no problem experimenting with new form-factors and it was hoping to create new markets with its devices. Even though many PC makers mocked Microsoft for its earlier hardware failures, every single one of them now builds a Surface Pro-like tablet. A tablet that can replace your laptop.

And in this new model, Microsoft positioned its hardware at the top. If you want a premium PC, Surface is the hardware you will likely consider but the company has also continued to leave plenty of room downstream as well. HP, Dell, and Lenovo have found that while Microsoft may define a market, they can compete at lower price points with high-quality hardware too.

Microsoft charges the highest price for its hardware but you can find better value with other brands for similarly configured products. This was Microsoft's goal: Sit at the top competing only with Apple, and let its partners fill out the PC portfolio.

Even though PC makers started to understand how the new PC landscape would operate, everything Microsoft does is politically sensitive. With each new product launch, each new iteration shipped, and each OS released, the company has to be careful. It is still heavily dependent on the partners that pay licensing fees to Microsoft each time they sell a PC.

Figuring out how to coexist with Surface wasn't the only adjustment that PC makers made during this time. They also started preparing for a future that might not include Windows. It is perhaps not coincidental that most major PC makers have adopted Chrome OS since the arrival of Surface. The fact that Chromebook sales have exploded, especially in the U.S. and Western Europe, is a thorn that is growing in Microsoft's side.

One PC maker said that it doubled-down on Chromebooks as soon as Surface Pro started becoming popular. This was a way to help diversify its offerings should the day come when Surface sells at volume. I have heard similar sentiments from multiple PC makers which see increasing their sales of Chromebooks as a way to push back against Microsoft.

But with Surface now generating over $4 billion in annual revenue for Microsoft, there is no doubt that it has been a successful venture for the company. The risks associated with competing against its own partners proved to be a worthwhile effort. And the market today, for all players involved, remains competitive with no major exits by any of the PC makers that were entrenched in this field prior to the launch of the first Surface tablets.

Chapter 17 - A Lumia, a Surface Pro, and a Surface Book Walk Into a Conference Room

"The Titanic missed the iceberg, we found a better path forward."

Following the successful launch of the Surface Pro 3, Microsoft moved over 3 million units in its 2015 fiscal year. And the Surface team found themselves as the popular kids at school once again on Microsoft's campus.

While renaming the brand was considered and moving away from being a PC company was once a possible strategy shift, all of that noise had fallen away. As Surface Pro 3 continued to sell well and the teething issues of the early hardware were ironed out, the conversation at Microsoft transitioned to how it could push the Surface brand forward.

This success removed a significant amount of weight from the collective shoulders of Panay and his team. The Surface brand was finally reaching the objectives of its original mission, to become the premium brand of the PC industry. But to fully reach that status, there was no time to rest and the team had other markets that it needed to tackle.

One of the defining moments of the Surface Pro 3 announcement was Microsoft comparing it to the MacBook Air. Microsoft wanted the world to know that its hardware was not just as good as Apple's but that it was better. It was lighter, it had a better display, and it was faster too. And the latest Type Cover was finally being recognized as a high-quality keyboard.

But if you want to be a premium brand and compete with Apple, it needs to be at all levels of the market. The Surface Pro was taking on Apple's "everyday" laptop. But Panay wanted to punch higher into Apple's lineup. He wanted to go after the MacBook Pro.

Apple's premium laptop has long been an industry benchmark and an icon. If you were a creative professional, the choice was almost always a MacBook Pro. Trying to beat what Apple had been building on for more than a decade would not be an easy challenge.

But Microsoft tackled this mountain with a new type of Surface called Surface Book. This detachable laptop went through many iterations and no idea was left off the table.

The challenge Microsoft faced in differentiating Surface Book was two-fold. It needed to attract the attention of the same people buying the MacBook Pro but it couldn't go too crazy with the hardware as it needed to be in the same price bracket as MacBook Pro. The goal was to get consumers and prosumers to cross-shop the two products.

And this was a key objective for Microsoft. Building hardware is one thing, but creating a premium brand is a challenge that cannot be discounted; simply having a high price does not establish that brand as premium. With Surface Pro 3, the premium narrative for Microsoft was starting to be established, but it was not until the Surface Book launched in 2015 that the company took the deep dive into the PC market that its PC maker partners had feared.

As with every release, developing Surface Book was as politically charged as the other hardware had been because the company was now not only building a tablet, but also a laptop. A laptop that was going to target existing PC products was a tougher sell to management, but they had something to help them win over not only insiders at the company but also the PC makers themselves.

With Surface Pro, Microsoft created a new market for high-powered tablets which allowed the company's partners to start selling new products in a new category.

The benefit that Microsoft has that no other company does in the PC space is that Microsoft's livelihood isn't dependent on selling hardware. The company makes the majority of its revenue from software and other services like Azure, so it can take risks in the hardware space that other companies cannot. Microsoft has the ability to fail in hardware without significant repercussions to its overall business.

Updating the Surface Pro at this point had become significantly easier. Once you have a product that is successful, you no longer need to think about changing the formula but simply refining it. Panay and his team knew this and focused on making Surface Pro 4 a refinement of the Surface Pro 3.

The idea of taking risks in the Pro line was no longer an option: the raw form factor had been created and the company would focus on iterative refinements for the next several versions of the hardware with no major design changes penciled in until 2019.

When it came to the Surface Book, Microsoft claimed that it would once again create a new market for the industry, just as it had done with Surface Pro. Despite hearing from PC makers that a laptop would not have the same impact as did Surface Pro, Microsoft persisted. And there wasn't much the company's partners could do; the new normal was that Microsoft was a competitor and also a business partner.

Panay and his team worked with Intel and others to create the foundation of the Surface Book and establish that an external GPU could be utilized seamlessly with Windows. If it were not for the external GPU, the Surface Book would simply be a larger Surface Pro with a metal keyboard.

But there was a problem that was eating away at Panay and it had nothing to do with Surface.

After the acquisition of Nokia's mobile assets, Microsoft was in a tough position. Its mobile market share was declining, and iOS and Android were quickly becoming the established players. These competitors had nearly removed Blackberry from the smartphone equation, and Microsoft wasn't sure about the future of its own mobile OS, called Windows Phone.

Microsoft was trying one more time with Windows Phone with the Lumia 950 and 950 XL, and it wanted Panay to announce the new handsets. But Panay didn't want to announce this hardware. He was afraid that these handsets would be associated with the Surface team.

In a meeting, Panay explicitly said he did not want to announce the Lumias. But he was told that it was best for the company to show its support for the Lumia handsets by announcing them alongside the new Surface hardware. Panay was not happy with this turn of events, and he would distance himself from the hardware when he announced it later that year.

Chapter 18 - Saving Windows

"It should have been a developer's dream, but they didn't care"

In July 2013, Terry Myerson stood atop his own burning platform. After running the company's mobile operations, he had been chosen to turn Windows around and save the platform that had long been the bedrock of the Redmond-based company. But Microsoft's desktop operating system was in shambles and its mobile platform was starting its long circling of the drain.

Microsoft had previously done some emergency triage work to save Windows 8 with the 8.1.x updates that returned the Start button and the Start menu. But the damage was done. After releasing the beloved Windows 7, Windows 8 had bombed. And it was up to Myerson to swing the pendulum back in the other direction.

One of the reasons that Myseron was chosen to run Windows is that he had previously led the team that made the tough decision to scrap Windows Mobile and build Windows Phone. While that mobile platform arrived too late to compete against iPhone and Android, it was well-liked by its users. So Myerson's goal for Windows was to pivot that desktop platform in a similar fashion.

With increased competition from Apple and Google, releasing another disastrous operating system was not a possibility; it was time to go back to the basics. Even though many saw this as Microsoft returning to a classic Windows design, more importantly, it meant going back to being transparent.

With each new Windows version, Microsoft liked to tout how the company had modernized the codebase. But the next version of Windows, called Windows 10, would be different. This time,

Microsoft had to adapt to Apple and Google's definition of modern, not its own. And modern operating systems were updated annually, not every 3 to 4 years. But at that time in 2013, Windows was not capable of sustaining frequent and substantial updates at scale.

The challenge for the engineers building Windows was to move the operating system to annual updates first, with the end goal being substantial updates twice a year. If Apple and Google shipped one major update per year, then Microsoft would ship two to show the world that Windows was even more flexible.

In 2014, Microsoft embarked on what would come to be known as One Core. The goal was to create one underlying operating system that would run on all the company's devices: PCs, mobile devices, Xbox, and more. This was a significant undertaking, but Microsoft felt that if it could truly unify the codebase, then developers could write an application once and have it run on any device powered by a Microsoft operating system.

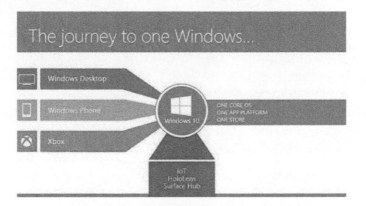

Microsoft's Goal for Creating 'One' Windows

The "write-once, run anywhere" dream—first popularized by Sun for its Java technologies—was alive and real inside of Microsoft. The marching orders were to make Windows the operating system of choice for developers. And if those building apps could use a single codebase to target hundreds of millions of users, Microsoft believed that its floundering app store would finally thrive.

But there was much more to Windows 10 than unifying, refactoring, and modernizing the codebase. It needed to be stable and reliable too. If the company hoped to launch the new OS in just two years, it would need a significant amount of testing. Microsoft had to ensure that it would not run into the same stability issues as Windows Vista or present the kinds of usability issues that had confused Windows 8 users.

Returning to its roots, Microsoft prepared to launch the largest beta testing channel in the company's history. And in September 2014, the Windows Insider program was born.

Spearheaded by Gabe Aul and Bill Karagounis, the Windows Insider program would start shipping pre-release versions of Windows 10, to anyone who showed an interest. It was instantly successful: A year after launching the Insider program, over 7 million people had signed up to test Windows 10.

Aside from getting feedback about basic UI changes and consumer features, the program served a greater purpose; it allowed Microsoft to learn how to update builds of Windows on-the-fly at what would become known as rapid-release. Of course, Microsoft already knew how to patch PCs: the firm updates over one billion Windows PCs on "Patch Tuesday," the second Tuesday of every month. But these patches only fixed issues; they did not add new features or functionality.

With the Insider program, Microsoft now had new insights into how several million people were using Windows 10. This allowed the company to troubleshoot issues at a scale that was not previously possible with any prior version of Windows. With a simple click of a button, a new build of Windows 10 can be shipped to millions of users who can then test compatibility and features and provide feedback to Microsoft, for free.

This new avenue for communication also was an olive branch to

Windows loyalists who were left out of the Windows 8 conversation. Microsoft was slowly transforming from an isolated company that knew what was best for its users to a company that was listening to feedback and adjusting its product accordingly with each new iteration.

While the Insider program provided usage and telemetry data to Microsoft at a significant volume and helped the company identify and troubleshoot the issues its automated testing did not detect, it was also a burden. Microsoft was unable to properly analyze all of the data it received, and it was becoming harder over time to find the useful signals in all of the noise.

To help counter this, Microsoft created a Feedback Hub app for Insiders, but it suffered from its own problems. Because issues are voted up or down by Insiders, popular feature requests would bubble to the top while isolated issues would remain buried in a sea of other complaints that would never be addressed. Microsoft has revamped how feedback is reviewed several times, but even to this day, the signal is still often lost inside all of the noise.

But the Insider program has largely been a net positive for Microsoft as the company pushed towards its goal of One Core for Windows. Microsoft eventually created similar Insider programs for much of the software the company ships, including such popular product lines as Office and Xbox.

But One Core has also proven to be a burden for Microsoft because it slowed development of its mobile platform and caused re-tooling of other aspects of its operations like Xbox. Ultimately, "write-once, run everywhere" was a dream that would never materialize. And the overhead it created while Microsoft brought various products in line is one that would contribute to the failure of its mobile operations while doing little to boost its fledgling app store.

While One Core was creating headaches for Microsoft's mobile platform, Windows 10 for PCs was moving full-steam ahead. And with each new build it shipped, Microsoft became more confident in the tooling it had created to rapidly ship new versions of Windows. Windows as a Service (WaaS) was born.

That name sparked its own controversy. With Microsoft's Office 365 performing exceptionally well, there was a natural fear amongst some users that the next version of Windows would be sold on a monthly or annual subscription, rather than via a more traditional lifetime license. Though that fear is understandable —the software giant has long sold Windows to corporations on a subscription basis via its Software Assurance licensing program—it has yet to turn into a reality for consumers.

One of Microsoft's goals with Windows 10 was to help the corporate world modernize its business practices. Prior to the release of Windows 10, organizations would update their operating system roughly every 6 or 8 years, but Microsoft wanted to change that to every 18 months.

This forced modernization would ultimately come back to haunt Microsoft as its corporate customers pushed back at the aggressive upgrade schedule. Since releasing the first version of Windows 10, the company has revised the lifecycle of each release from 18 to 24 and then eventually to 30 months for its corporate users. Many believe it will continue pushing out the lifecycle going forward as well.

Teething issues aside, Windows 10, with the help of the Insider program, achieved its goal of overhauling the delivery mechanisms for major updates and making the operating system more flexible moving forward.

As the company approached the initial Windows 10 release, Panay and his team knew what needed to be done. Windows 10, like Windows 8 before it, needed "hero" hardware. The decision was made that after the dust had settled from the release of the new operating system and the early pains of day-zero updates were over, the company would release new Surface hardware in the same way that it had done with Windows 8.

Windows 10 was released to the world on July 29, 2015, and the early indications were that Myerson and his team were on the right path. Windows 10 was following in the footsteps of Windows 7, not Windows 8.

Twenty four hours after Microsoft shipped the operating system, it announced that 14 million devices were already running Windows 10. While this number is impressive, it was inflated by those in the Insider program, as they simply received a new update in late July and were then included in the 14 million figure. A month after launch, there were around 80 million PCs running the operating system. By October of 2015, the number crossed 100 million. And by January of 2016, it hit 200 million devices.

Internally, the company had a public counter showing the adoption rate of the OS. With each new download, the number would grow higher and with millions downloading each day in the first few weeks after the release, these numbers were being released to the press as they helped paint a picture of momentum for Windows 10.

Like all good things, Microsoft quickly shut down the site showing the adoption rate as it was becoming a liability to the company. With a few simple messages to sources at Microsoft during the first couple weeks, I could find out the exact adoption rate of the OS and plot its course to estimate when major milestones, such as 100 million, would be reached. This became an issue for Microsoft not only because it didn't want any news about "slowing adoption" in the early days. But those trying to predict the company's earnings could use this data as well.

Myerson, perhaps foolishly, made lofty promises about the OS being on one billion devices within three years. But the company would ultimately come up short of that goal; the failure of the mobile platform significantly impacted the growth rate of Windows 10.

By early 2018, Windows 10 adoption had stalled out at around 670 million devices. The company said that adoption was "nearly" 700 million multiple times over the next several months, leading to questions and speculation about growth. But the reason why the figure stopped growing rapidly is that the company had stopped counting virtual machines as part of its user base after Myerson left the company. By removing VMs from the count, the active user base dropped around 9%.

Even with Windows 10 receiving high praise from reviewers when compared to Windows 8, the lack of app store usage continued and still haunted Microsoft. The company had hoped that by aligning the basics of all of its platforms with One Core that the app store would flourish.

After all, Microsoft was making it easier for developers to build apps for all of its platforms. And adoption was finally pushing in the right direction, for the desktop at least. But as time passed and the reality sank in that its mobile platform, including its expensive Nokia assets, was going to flop, the company made fundamental changes to its strategy that broke the promise of One Core.

Not long after the release of Windows 10, Microsoft saw that the writing was on the wall for the Windows Store. The company made the tough decision to make it easier to bring existing desktop and web applications into its store. But by doing so, it broke the ability to have all store apps potentially run on any of its devices; the One Core dream was dead.

This app store, now called Microsoft Store, still has a long way to go. But it's at least in a more respectable place today with big-name applications like Spotify and Apple's iTunes being offered. Looking back, it seems that the decision to abandon the One Core principals was the right move.

By 2017, Microsoft was ready to make its next big move for Windows, with the company finally recognizing that the glory days of the platform were now behind it. Moving forward, it would simply maintain the status quo so that the OS could ride off into the sunset for the next couple of decades.

As part of this shift, Myerson would exit the company, having successful pivoted Windows into a sustainable platform. The operating system would now shift focuses to make sure that it meets the ongoing challenges of the enterprise first and deliver consumer features second.

But back in 2015, the future of Windows 10 was not as certain as it is today. The company was still trying to make it the best OS for every computing device. And to showcase the operating system, Panay and his team were going to build the best Windows laptop the world had ever seen.

Chapter 19 - The Hardware High Note

"We did it, we got everything ready at the same time; it was a miracle"

On September 14, 2015, Microsoft sent out invites to what many now consider to be its all-time best hardware event. If you are a fan of Microsoft hardware, this was the peak.

Microsoft invited press and analysts to an event at the Skylight at Moynihan in New York City. While the seating was much better than previous venues, the presentation got off to a very rough start.

Media Invite Sent to the Press

For the press, Internet connectivity is key. For this particular event, the Wi-Fi collapsed under the pre-event traffic, causing serious problems for the bloggers and journalists who were trying to live-blog the event or just ship images back to headquarters for publication.

Because the Wi-Fi was not working, everyone was switching over to cellular devices for connectivity. But the signal inside the building was weak and the cellular connections were dropping as well. Microsoft scrambled to try and fix the connectivity so that the press could communicate to the outside world but it was an embarrassing display for a technology company.

The connection issue reached the point that Mary Jo Foley—who lived nearby in New York City—literally left the building. She felt it was better to watch the live stream at home and cover the announcement from there than being next to the stage because it was impossible to file stories. A staffer from Waggener Edstrom chased after Mary Jo as she left the building and was able to convince her to return after promising wired connectivity.

We later learned that this was the last event at this location before the building would be gutted and remodeled. While Microsoft took the blame, it was the venue's Wi-Fi that had collapsed under the load of the event, something Microsoft did not have control over at the time. This was a hard lesson for Microsoft and all subsequent events have had wired connectivity for bloggers and journalists.

When the show was ready to begin, Terry Myerson took the stage to highlight the momentum behind Windows 10 and to lay the foundation for Microsoft's new hardware. While most people remember this presentation for the Surface Book announcement, it was also where the company announced Surface Pro 4, two new Lumia handsets, and the second-generation Microsoft Band wearable, plus the HoloLens Developer hardware shipment date.

Demonstrated by Lindsey Matese, the second-generation Microsoft Band was more ergonomic and more functional than its predecessor. It was also the last fitness wearable that the company would ever sell. Microsoft Band 3 was canceled late in its development cycle after the company came to the conclusion that its hardware efforts in anything other than Surface and Xbox were coming up short.

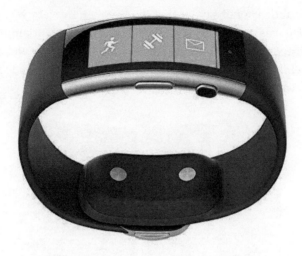

Microsoft Band 2

Much like Windows Phone, Microsoft Band had attracted a small but dedicated user base. But the devices had serious build quality problems, a common theme for the hardware announced at this event. The rubber straps would disintegrate after a few months of heavy use, which was a serious issue for a device that was supposed to be worn on your wrist.

But the Band wasn't Panay's problem. This was just the opening act for his announcements, and as Myerson and Matese progressed through their presentations, Panay paced, mentally walking through the steps he would take on stage. Where he would announce two Surface products plus an unrelated product that he didn't want associated with his name or his Surface team.

Taking the stage, Panay dove into Windows 10 momentum but immediately started to distance himself from the Lumia team. Noting that he had only been working with them for a short while, he said that he supported their vision for the direction of Microsoft's mobile platform.

It was a subtle way of saying that the Lumia hardware was not his design. He was the person making the announcement and he said he supported the vision and the technology of the team who created it. But behind the scenes, and even with the press, he made it clear that this was not his hardware.

Lumia 950

In showing off Windows 10 Mobile, Panay noted that Continuum—which let you connect the phone to a monitor, keyboard, and mouse—would only get better with the Universal apps that were coming to the Windows Store.

At that time, Windows 10 had just launched and it was being installed millions of times each day. And Microsoft assumed that as adoption increased, developers would jump on board and would start building apps for the Windows Store.

Unfortunately for Microsoft, those apps would not arrive and this would be the last high-end Lumia that it would ever announce.

But to change the tune, quite literally with AC/DC's "Thunderstruck" blasting throughout the building, Panay unveiled the Surface Pro 4 with a child-like smirk on his face. This was an obvious upgrade. The Surface team took the much-loved Surface Pro 3— 98% of owners said they would recommend the device—made the display a bit bigger, shaved away the sides to make it thinner, and increased the performance.

Microsoft Surface Pro 4

Notably, this was also when Microsoft introduced the new branding for the hardware. The new Surface PCs were branded with "Microsoft" not "Surface." Against the wishes of Panay and the Surface team, Microsoft had decided that its own corporate brand should be used.

The passion that Panay presents on stage when he announces his own products is oftentimes described as contagious. This level of energy was not present when he announced the Lumia 950. But once he moved past that and announced Surface Pro 4, he was back into his traditional form of speaking.

Panay noted that Surface Pro 4's larger display was all about making the device more productive. Microsoft was becoming quite comfortable with making productivity cool. And even though this idea was previously shunned internally, the message was working with Surface and there was no going back at this point.

And Panay was not one to hold back from acknowledging market realities. When announcing the Lumia 950, he joked about how all the specs had been leaked and smirked when he said everyone had been writing about them for weeks. But when he pulled the new Surface Pen out of his pocket, he joked about how Apple had announced a pencil without an eraser but he had a pen with one.

At the time of the announcement, Panay noted that 50% of Surface Pro 3 users were using the Surface Pen. Microsoft initially shipped a Surface Pen with the Surface Pro 4 in the box but it would later ship iterations of the hardware that did not include the Pen. By the time the company started selling the next Surface Pro, it would stop including Surface Pen altogether after it was determined that actual use of the pen was significantly lower than 50%.

With Surface Pro 4 behind him, Panay shifted the presentation back to familiar messaging: He wanted to change the industry. And while you could argue that Surface Pro had done just that, doing so with a laptop was a much harder challenge.

"What if we could do for laptops, what we did for tablets?" he asked rhetorically. It was a bold goal considering that the company's PC maker partners had been building laptops for decades.

But the Surface Book was built to do one thing: Knock the MacBook Pro off of its perch. Microsoft wanted to show that it could compete with the best laptop maker in the world, Apple.

Surface Book was not meant to be a mass-market device. Instead, it was designed to be the hero of the laptop category. The defining feature of the Surface Book was that the display could be detached and used as a tablet. When attached to its keyboard base, Surface Book would gain additional battery life plus, optionally, a dedicated graphics card as well.

Surface Book

This was not an easy technological task, and it required the hardware and software to work in perfect harmony. If the GPU was being utilized, the display could not be detached because Windows could crash. So Microsoft had to figure out how to seamlessly switch between the GPU and the integrated Intel graphics and do so in a way that would not interrupt the user's workflow.

The Surface Book announcement was a turning point for the brand. While Surface Pro 3 had shown that Microsoft could build a device that customers would love, Surface Book showed that the company was ready to branch out from its tablet roots and go after other markets as well.

With each new release, Microsoft engaged in the same politically charged in-fighting about upsetting its PC maker partners. Ultimately, it would come down to the fact that Microsoft wanted to be in charge of its own destiny in the PC space. And though its partners still sold millions of PCs each year, it needed to ensure that there would always be a high-quality premium PC brand as well.

As Panay left the stage, Satya Nadella came on to show his commitment to the brand and the direction in which Microsoft was heading. But what neither knew at that time was that Intel would not live up to a promise it had made. And while the Surface Book was ready to launch from Microsoft's perspective, it was not actually ready for customers.

The following day, Microsoft held a smaller meeting with some of the attendees from the previous day's presentation. There, Panay and others from his team talked more intimately about the hardware and gave reporters a chance to ask additional questions. Panay again pointed out that the Lumia 950 was not his phone and that it was made by a team he had subsequently been assigned to lead.

As the smaller meeting came to an end, it felt like Christmas in October. Microsoft started handing out the review units and everyone received a Microsoft Band 2 wearable, a Lumia 950 smartphone, a Surface Pro 4, and a Surface Book. To this day, it's the most hardware I have ever received at any event from any vendor.

One thing worth pointing out is that the Surface Book review box was completely white with no product photography or branding. At that time, I had assumed this was done to protect the identity of the contents inside from leaks. But I later learned it was because the final box design was not completed in time for shipping the review hardware.

The fact that such a detail had been overlooked foreshadowed the road ahead for Microsoft. The company was about to walk into a minefield of trouble with its new hardware.

Chapter 20 - A Hard Computer Science Problem

"If this was a boxing match, the towel would have been tossed in round one"

Every iteration of hardware that Microsoft released has had issues of some kind. Surface Pro 3 suffered from a serious Wi-Fi bug that would not let it connect to some networks and other devices had overheating problems or issues with adapters and the like.

Building hardware is difficult in the best of circumstances. But Microsoft was about to learn a very important lesson when it comes to pushing the boundaries and taking risks with new chipsets.

New hardware issues are common from every vendor and Surface is no different. There were consistent quality issues with early devices and the exteriors were easily scratched. But this would all pale in comparison to what happened with Surface Book.

In May 2015, Microsoft released a smaller version of its Surface tablet called the Surface 3. The device was the spiritual successor to Surface RT but instead of using an ARM-based CPU, it utilized Intel's low-end Atom processor.

By moving away from ARM, Microsoft could build a smaller device, albeit one with a bit less battery life, that had none of Windows RT's compatibility baggage. At that time, Intel was still trying to figure out how to scale down its processors while also maintaining performance and matching ARM's battery life. And it thought it had finally found the answer with "Cherry Trail," the codename for this generation of Atom processors.

Surface 3

Unlike with other new Surface devices, Microsoft did not hold a press event to announce Surface 3. Because the tablet was not a flagship product, it was soft-launched and the company gave the press embargoed materials ahead of the announcement.

The smaller device was targeted at the education segment and had a lower entry price, but it was plagued not by bad hardware, for a change, but by bad branding.

When Microsoft was figuring out which components would go into Surface 3, it asked Intel to change the branding of its Atom line of processors. Microsoft was rightfully concerned that the wave of low-end netbook PCs that had been released a few years earlier had ruined the Atom brand. And that users would perceive it as being sub-par and not up to everyday computing tasks.

Netbooks were the original ultra-budget-friendly Windows PCs. They had low prices, and underpowered Atom processors to match, and they flooded the market, tarnishing the Windows brand as they did so. The problem was that the hardware was powerful enough only for very basic tasks and the PCs made standard productivity applications painful to use. While the dream of ultra-cheap Windows PCs came and went quickly, Microsoft had a bit more luck with the Surface 3.

The device sold well in education and also paved a path for Microsoft to create a low-cost product within the confines of the premium PC market. Ultimately, the product achieved its goals for the brand. But it wasn't a massive success, in part because of the stigma of the Atom brand.

Even with its modest success, Microsoft would hold off on building another smaller Surface device until Intel created another low-end chipset that distanced itself from the Atom brand.

But the bet with the Surface 3 paid off, and Microsoft had shipped the first Cherry Trail device and had benefitted from being able to leverage that in its marketing. The company hoped to replicate this marketing success by taking another, bigger bet, by shipping the Surface Book with Intel's newest, but untested, "Skylake" chipset.

The days after the Surface Pro 4 and Surface Book announcement should have been an exciting time for Microsoft. The company was about to launch its first new form factor since the original Surface Pro, and it was a product that was going to give Microsoft a complete portfolio to challenge Apple in the premium space.

But there was one problem, and it was a big one. Skylake was not ready for Windows 10. And Microsoft was venturing down a path that would have executives fearing they may lose their jobs over greenlighting a product that was going to tarnish the Surface band they had so delicately built over three generations of products.

Microsoft knew about the problems before launching the hardware. Some of them were related to Skylake's inability to properly move the PC into a power management mode called sleep.

Windows 10 would try to put Surface into a low power state to conserve battery life while being transported, but it would fail to do so. The challenge of putting the device to sleep would become a meme among enthusiasts when a Microsoft support rep inadvisedly called it a "hard computer science problem." Since that unfortunate event, every issue related to Surface going forward would then be jokingly referred to as a hard computer science problem.

Microsoft worked with Intel to figure out how to overcome these challenges. And they thought that it would be a simple fix. Intel had told Microsoft that it could have the problem patched with a software update about a week after the release of the hardware. With this promise, Microsoft pushed forward and announced Surface Book and Surface Pro 4.

The first hardware was handed out to the press and the issues became obvious almost immediately.

There were problems with both Surface Book and Surface Pro 4 related to power management that created the term "hot-bag," a phrase that would grow to irk Microsoft even more than "lappability."

The problem was that when a Surface Book or Surface Pro 4 was put to sleep, it would quietly turn back on and drain the battery. If this happened in a bag, it would heat it up; this problem would plague Microsoft for months.

It's bad enough for users to experience this kind of thing with PCs they had only owned for a few weeks or months but it was plaguing expensive, newly-bought hardware that had been sitting on store shelves. There were many documented incidents where a customer would buy a new Surface Book and upon opening, find a completely flat battery: It had "hot-bagged" inside of its box.

After finding the PC like this, the user would charge it and turn it on for what should have been a first-boot experience. But instead, it would start in a special recovery mode that made it appear as if the hardware had been refurbished or was otherwise not new. This resulted in returns of the device and low customer satisfaction scores.

For months, Microsoft tried to resolve the hot bag issue with multiple updates. But it persisted long enough after the launch that it severely tarnished the momentum that Surface had experienced following the launch event. Had this been the only problem with the two new devices, Panay and his team would have slept much better. But the laundry list of tragedies was significant enough that

Microsoft CFO Amy Hood lashed out at Panay during an internal meeting and said that the secrecy of building new hardware should never trump thorough testing before a product is released.

Worse for Microsoft, not long after its new CEO, Satya Nadella, took over the company, he made sweeping organizational structural changes that resulted in it shifting the way it developed software. As a result, the company had fired a significant portion of its quality assurance teams. With new hardware being released that had significant stability issues, one wonders whether Microsoft might have found these issues before launch had it not fired these testers.

There were other problems.

At its launch, Surface Book did not include a software shortcut to release its "clipboard" display from the keyboard base. If a user needed to detach the clipboard, they pressed a special hardware key on the keyboard base; Microsoft's engineers were so confident that this would always work that it was the only way one could detach the clipboard.

One of the advantages of this clipboard design was that a user could detach the display, flip it around, and reattach it "backward." This made it easier to draw on the display and have it act more like a canvas. But while reviewing the Surface Book, Peter Bright of Ars Technica put his device in this configuration and it became stuck; the device had not even launched yet and the only option for disconnecting the clipboard display had already failed.

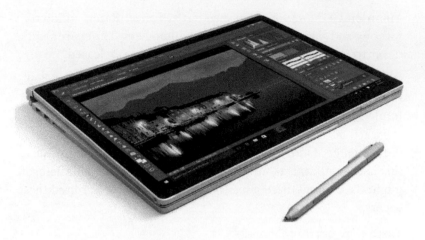

Surface Book in Canvas Mode

Microsoft sent Bright an internal software program called "Samurai" that ran a script that unlocked the display. In a future update, Microsoft included the software unlock for the display so everyone could take advantage of it.

Surface Book's launch issues were numerous and included problems with the clipboard display randomly detaching, the power button becoming unresponsive after driver updates, Wi-Fi disconnecting, and the keyboard becoming unresponsive as well. Surface Pro 4 had similar issues and Intel released driver updates which would attempt to resolve many issues but introduced a new fan favorite, display driver crashes.

Even though Surface Book had an NVIDIA graphics chipset, it would often use Intel's display driver when the additional power of a discrete graphics chip was not needed. The problem was that the Intel driver would crash frequently on both of the new Surface PCs. And that would cause Windows to crash; the result was that consumers returned these devices at a higher than the anticipated rate.

Microsoft's problems would peak in August 2017, well after it had already fixed the issues, when Consumer Reports pulled its recommended status for all Surface products. The publication noted that 25% of the Surface devices purchased by its readers would break by the end of the second year of ownership. This was a serious blow to any momentum Microsoft had with its brand.

The original launch of the Surface RT was a financial disaster. But the release of Surface Book was inflicting serious damage to the brand that Panay and his team had fought so hard to create. Inside the company, it was a five-alarm fire to figure out how they could resolve issues with the hardware.

In the 18 months following the Surface Book and Surface Pro 4 release, Microsoft would release a significant number of firmware updates that eventually did make the devices substantially more reliable. Several years later, when vulnerabilities called Spectre and Meltdown were found with Intel's chipsets, a Microsoft executive joked that patching these problems with Windows Update wasn't an issue since Surface and Skylake had paved the way.

The challenges that Microsoft faced after taking a risk by releasing a premium product with an untested chipset taught a simple lesson: Launch when you are ready, not when you can be first. It's a stigma that has followed the brand ever since, much like the hard lessons of ordering too much inventory for the Surface RT.

But this wouldn't be the end of issues for Microsoft. Intel has had difficulty shipping its upcoming 10nm chipset, called "Ice Lake," which Microsoft has planned to use in many upcoming products. These Intel delays mean that Microsoft will need to re-work its designs to utilize an interim chip or wait for Intel to possibly ship Ice Lake as late as 2020.

Because Intel dictates when Microsoft can improve the performance of its hardware, the software giant is in a bind. It can leave its current products in the market longer and face stagnating sales as the products age. Or it can push forward with the Intel's interim chip which was not originally in its plans so that it can update its hardware faster and keep sales at higher volumes.

One thing is for certain. The issues Intel is facing with Ice Lake are serious and there is a sense of deja-vu inside the walls of Microsoft's Redmond campus; it will not let this new chipset become Skylake V2.

Chapter 21 - The Studio

"The iMac was sitting still, so we made a desktop that could move"

Even though the Surface Book launch was a disaster, it did pave the way for new types of hardware. And it showed that Microsoft was serious about building a complete portfolio of devices to compliment Surface Pro.

The challenge was that with each new product that Microsoft would create, Panay wanted to define a new product category. He wanted a Surface device to be the hero in every channel where a PC was sold. And that meant setting the bar as high as possible where form and function take priority over cost and construction.

Venturing into the desktop PC space was a natural evolution for the Surface brand. Building a desktop PC is quite a bit different than building a tablet or detachable laptop as the traditional form factor has been around for decades. But there was room for improvement.

One thing was clear when the Surface Studio was announced: Panay and his team were targeting the aging iMac, and they had a formula that Apple was refusing to embrace. During the press announcement, Panay drilled home the point that this machine was for everyone, but that it also extracted the creativity from the individual.

In Cupertino, Apple had slowly been extending the release cycles between its desktop updates. And fans of the iMac, which is an all-in-one PC, were waiting anxiously for a significant refresh. By September 2018, Apple had yet to change the formula for the iMac. It refused to add any touch-input functionality, including the Touchbar it had previously added to the MacBook Pro. This created an opening for Microsoft to step in and steal a bit of thunder.

Surface Studio development was quite literally a family affair. Microsoft loves to rapidly prototype hardware using office materials and anything else the Surface team can get its hands on, and Ralf Groene's daughter helped design Surface Studio during a summer internship. Not a bad gig for an upcoming industrial designer.

Early Surface Studio Mockup Shown at Ignite 2018

There are two key components of the Studio, the screen and the hinge. While the computer portion of the Studio is important as well, compared to the engineering efforts of the display and the arm supporting the display, that was child's play.

Surface Studio has the best display of any Surface product in existence and it is quite possibly the best PC display in the industry. Microsoft invested more time and effort into perfecting the glass and LCD than with previous products. And it came at a significant cost as well.

Surface Studio had a starting price of $2999 and when I asked Microsoft following the announcement how much it would cost just to sell the display, they quoted a figure of about $2000. Knowing this, you can understand why Microsoft has yet to offer a standalone Surface display: The price would be too high. And the

Surface Studio was expected to sell in a low volume, so creating a standalone display might cut into the sales of expensive PC. Microsoft was worried that this would undercut the value and messaging of the product as well.

As is usually the case with Surface products, the Surface Studio's hinge is a key defining feature. Groene worked with his team and burned quite a bit of midnight oil to come up with a solution that would allow the display to articulate without needing a locking mechanism. Microsoft refers to it as a zero-gravity design.

The spring setup inside the Surface Studio had a significant number of revisions. Models where the user would have to press a button to unlock the display, much like the Surface Book, were explored. But in an effort to create as little friction as possible to move between desktop mode and canvas mode, that idea was scrapped.

This is a specific point in Surface's history where you can see Panay and his team not settling for the easy solution. The team could have used the "muscle-wire" setup from Surface Book for Surface Studio and shipped the product more quickly. But instead, they created a new solution that has become the hallmark of the product.

The company had two options for display articulation. There is the hinge setup that made its way to production that we know today, but there was also a prototype that had more flexibility.

When pulling the screen down into what Microsoft calls canvas mode, the articulation of the display becomes fixed. But Microsoft also experimented with screens that could articulate forward and backward while in canvas mode. Ultimately, it determined that this additional flexibility made it harder to use the Studio.

While previous Surface devices had routinely been leaked by myself or others, Surface Studio was a rare instance in which Microsoft leaked the product itself. No, not through a poorly-built staging site like Xbox had done so many times before, or by an executive accidentally revealing specifications as with HoloLens. Instead,

Microsoft published the patents for the hardware months ahead of its reveal.

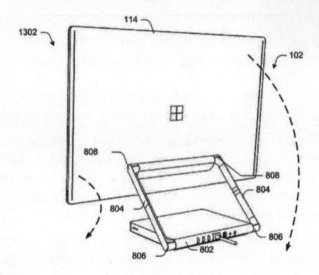

Surface Studio Patent

In February 2016, a Microsoft patent for a "modular PC" appeared in the US Patent and Trademark database that did not simply hint at a desktop PC, but showed off the device in nearly-final form.

Microsoft announced Surface Studio on October 26 at a Windows 10 event in New York City. It was at this event that Panay revealed a bit of his child-like joy for building this hardware. When he unveiled the device in front of a crowd of journalists and thousands viewing the live stream online, he broke from his mold of calm and calculated to reveal his inner-pride in the new PC.

For someone who rehearses diligently, breaking from his calm and collected charisma provided a bit of insight into the immense passion he and his team put into the hardware. Time and time again I have been asked if Panay's stage presence is an act. But I firmly believe that on stage or in the office, there is no difference in the

131

way he carries and presents himself to employees or to fans based on the interviews conducted for this book.

Surface Studio

At the announcement, Microsoft also showed off what it hoped would be the next great peripheral for Surface, called Surface Dial. The puck-sized device can sit on the Surface Studio display and it allows the user to manipulate content like copy/paste or adjust contrast in Adobe PhotoShop. The goal was to make this peripheral the artist dream device.

Surface Dial

Surface Dial played a significant role in making Surface Studio something other than an overly-large all-in-one PC. It was the combination of Surface Pen, Surface Dial, an articulating multi-touch display, and Windows 10 working in harmony to create what Microsoft envisioned as the best digital canvas on the planet.

On the bottom of the Surface Dial is a rubber pad that is designed to sit on the Surface Studio display. But because the display could be articulated in many different positions, it had to be sticky, but not stick. Surface Dial was designed to also be useful when off of the display as well.

The treading on the bottom of Surface Dial was refined more times than the Surface Studio hinge or the display. Granted, it's much easier to print a rubber pad with a new texture than it is to manufacture a new PC case. But it's still a point worth making that Surface Dial wasn't simply an afterthought. It received as much attention and care as the rest of the hardware.

While the display, hinge, and exterior of the Surface Studio made a bold impression, Microsoft neutered its own success by using relatively low-performance internals for the PC itself. Nearly every review of Surface Studio praised Microsoft's ambitions with the display and hinge but chastised the company for using the previous years' graphics card and processor.

Worse, the storage was not entirely solid state, which significantly impacted performance when the device was used for heavy-duty applications like video editing or CAD (computer-aided design). Even though the hard drives had some SSD capacity, the older-style platter storage was noisy and the thermals required a constantly-spinning fan. For a device that started at $2999, it was a marvel of engineering, but it also came up short of the expected ultra-premium experience.

But what Surface Studio did do for Microsoft and the PC industry is once again raise the bar, in this case on what a desktop computer could be. And it was capable of challenging Apple's dominant iMac as well, though the iMac still far outsells Surface Studio. But sales superiority was never the goal. Microsoft set out to build a better iMac and it very clearly achieved this objective.

Chapter 22 - The Pawn for Windows 10 S

"It was the product people wanted with an annoying pop-up"

For years, Surface fans wanted Microsoft to build a laptop that could compete with Apple's popular and innovative MacBook Air. While the company initially said the only laptop that it would build would be the high-end Surface Book, those plans would change once Terry Myerson found a reason to release a less sophisticated device.

If you ever find yourself with a master key to the Microsoft offices, there is one place you should head to first. It's referred to as the "vault." This is where the company keeps its designs for hardware projects that have been shelved for various reasons.

When it came time to build a Surface-branded laptop, this device already existed in the vault; all the team had to do was prepare it for release. This shouldn't be that big of a surprise, as the Surface team often explores form factors and shelves quite a few projects, like watches and other pocketable devices, all the time.

But it was also a bit of a hard sell internally to ship a basic laptop. For years, Microsoft had pitched the notion that it had a tablet that could replace your laptop. By releasing a traditional laptop, this would shoot Surface Pro's legacy right in the hinge.

Surface Laptop was also a pawn in an internal political battle. It was released with Windows 10 S, a stripped down version of Windows that would fail to gain traction and ultimately be downgraded in importance only a year later.

Microsoft held an education-focused event in May 2017 where the company launched a refreshed initiative to go after a market that was being stolen away by Chromebooks.

To help push back against Chromebooks, which were known for their low cost, simplicity, and ease of management, Terry Myerson and his team conjured up Windows 10 S, a new version of Windows that would only run Windows Store apps.

The idea was that by only allowing Store apps to run with Windows 10 S, the system would be more secure, faster, and easier to manage. If this sounds familiar, it's because it's a retread of the Windows RT playbook. But Microsoft was promising this time that it had the right formula and that the Windows Store was finally in a position to support this computing model.

The problem was that Microsoft was never able to truly convince the general population that Windows 10 S was actually better than traditional Windows 10. Even though the company showed onstage at the event how the first boot was faster by 15 or more seconds, the performance narrative was never fully vetted by the company or the press, and the entire thing was a conjured up mess of confusion for consumers.

If you tried to run a traditional desktop application with Windows 10 S, you were blocked by the system. The pop-up notification explained that you could run this application if you first upgraded the PC to Windows 10 Pro, which was free for a limited time. Most consumers simply upgraded because they needed to run a particular app. But they did so without understanding that they were leaving Windows 10 S.

For the most part, consumers simply did not understand Windows 10 S. This version of Windows looked like "real" Windows 10, it functioned like Windows 10, but it couldn't download or install the same desktop applications that users had relied on for decades. Upgrading to Windows 10 Pro defeated the entire purpose of Windows 10 S.

In the first half of 2018, Microsoft changed Windows 10 S into a "mode" for mainstream versions of Windows 10 like Windows 10

Home and Pro. The idea is that any iteration of Windows 10 could be run in a locked-down S mode that would only allow Store apps to be installed. But what the company was really doing was moving Windows 10 S, or S mode, to the backburner. Today, with Myerson gone, S mode is no longer a focus. Microsoft's dream of having a version of Windows that only runs apps from the Windows Store is dead, again.

But before the death of Windows 10 S, Panay announced Surface Laptop at the education event. The product was the first to deviate from the traditional Surface messaging, as you'll see.

Panay loves to work the crowd during his presentations. One thing he has done time and time again is to find someone in the audience using a Mac or other brand of PC and give them one of his latest creations. Prior to the event, Paul and I saw Panay walking around and scanning the audience, and we both knew what he was doing when he approached the person sitting next to us at the event; he had found his target.

He approached the woman sitting next to us and gave her a Surface Laptop. While he did this, I managed to take a selfie that was captured on the live-stream of the event and broadcast to hundreds of thousands of people. It is a high-water mark for the embarrassing act of taking a selfie.

Prior to Surface Laptop being announced, the Surface brand was about a traditional-looking device that morphed into something greater. Surface Pro was a tablet that could be a laptop, Surface Book was a laptop with a detachable display that could be used as a tablet, and Surface Studio was a desktop PC that was also a drafting board. But Surface Laptop was simply a laptop with an Alcantara cover around the keyboard. It was also the first Surface product to offer color options as well, with Platinum, Gold, Burgundy, and Cobalt versions available.

Burgundy Surface Laptop

Surface Laptop was being used as a pawn to help sell Windows 10 S because Microsoft feared that if it didn't build premium hardware that came pre-installed with 10 S, then none of its PC maker partners would take this risk either.

Microsoft's fears were justified. In the year following the Surface Laptop release, it was the only premium PC to offer Windows 10 S. Lenovo, Dell, HP, and other PC makers only offered low-end, education-oriented PCs with the system. Surface Laptop was a casualty in Myerson's battle to make the Windows Store a success.

Microsoft never released figures on the Windows 10 S adoption rate for obvious reasons. But internal documentation I viewed stated that 60% of those Surface Laptop owners switched to Windows 10 Pro within the first 24 hours. Of those who didn't switch in the first seven days, 83% stuck with Windows 10 S.

Even with the Windows 10 S awkwardness, Surface Laptop finally delivered the product many had been asking the company to build for years: A standard laptop, made of premium materials, excellent build quality, and a high-resolution display. Once again, Apple had been slow to upgrade its aging MacBook Air to a more modern design, and Microsoft hoped to capitalize on this opening in the market.

But one thing was certain with this release, Microsoft was getting significantly better at shipping new devices with fewer issues. While Surface Laptop was less complex than Surface Book or Surface Studio, it received far fewer Issues Per Week (IPU) after its first month of availability than did its the other products.

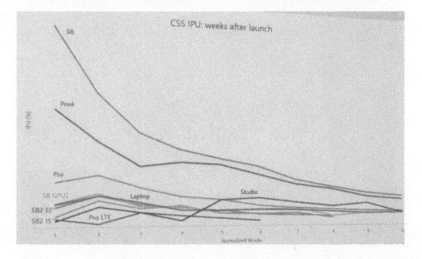

Issues Per Week Chart Shown at Ignite 2018

With the release of Surface Laptop, Microsoft felt like it finally had a PC for every person. This was the final building block to taking on Apple in the premium PC space, at every price point, and in every product category. Surface hardware could finally be cross-shopped with everything that Apple was selling.

Chapter 23 - Larger is Better and Harder

"A good marketer can hide reality, a good reporter will find the truth"

Microsoft, at its heart, is an enterprise software and services company. While it has a few successful consumer ventures like the Xbox and, to a lesser extent, Surface, the company makes the majority of its revenue from its corporate customers. And it is here that the firm made its next big Surface push.

In July 2012, Microsoft acquired Perceptive Pixel Inc (PPI), which was founded by Jeff Han. The company is best known for creating the CNN Magic Wall that was heavily used during the presidential election coverage that year.

The PPI acquisition was spearheaded by Stevie Bathiche. But even with Han's expertise and assistance, Microsoft had significant trouble building out the first generation device based on PPI's technology, called Surface Hub.

Microsoft announced Surface Hub on January 21, 2015 at the Windows 10 event at which it also revealed the first HoloLens. Cleverly, it was hidden in plain sight throughout that event.

Satya Nadella standing in front of Surface Hub 1

Microsoft used the Surface Hub throughout its presentation and eventually announced the hardware as its own vision of what an all-in-one conference room collaboration solution could be. It included everything but the kitchen sink and cost as much as a kitchen remodel as well.

The first generation Surface Hub shipped in two display sizes, 55-inches and 84-inches. Each was based on Intel Core i5 processors but had different graphics chipsets. The smaller unit used an Intel HD 4600 integrated graphics controller with a display running at 1920 x 1080 and the 84-inch version used an NVIDIA Quadro K2200 graphics processor.

The displays both supported a 120hz refresh rate and had 100 multi-touch input capabilities. Toss in 8GB of RAM, up to six USB ports, two webcams, and all the input ports you could imagine and you had a highly flexible, conference room collaboration solution that supported multiple users.

Though the Surface Hub was announced about three years after

Microsoft acquired PPI, it may have been a bit premature as there were some significant hiccups to come.

In July 2015, Microsoft opened up Surface Hub pre-orders with prices set at $6999 for the 55-inch version and the $19,999 for the 84-inch model. The company said it would start to ship Surface Hub in September that year but it would ultimately miss its deadline, twice.

Soon after it started accepting pre-orders, Microsoft realized it had made a huge mistake. Its logistics were not in place, the manufacturing process was turning out to be significantly harder than expected, and the company had to delay the device by four months, to January 1, 2016.

In the enterprise world, this kind of delay typically isn't a deal breaker as these companies look out to the horizon for planning purposes. But for Microsoft, the delay was yet another black eye for Surface. But if one delay is embarrassing, what does two mean?

In December 2016, Microsoft had to delay the release of the hardware once again, pushing it back to a vague Q1 2017 release. But Microsoft was also forced to raise the prices of the hardware by $2000 each because of an unexpected increase in the cost of its components. So the 55-inch Surface Hub would now cost $8,999 and the 84-inch model was now priced at $21,999.

Microsoft did honor the original prices for any customers that pre-ordered before the price increase. But it was an embarrassing setback for a company that was trying to prove that it could build not only consumer hardware but also enterprise-grade products as well.

Even with the price hikes, Surface Hub still offered a good value to those building new or retrofitted conference rooms; competing systems can run into the many tens of thousands of dollars. PPI's original device cost about $80,000, for example. So Microsoft was able to not only cut the price significantly but also increase the value of the hardware by making the software integrate better into the Windows ecosystem.

Despite these setbacks, Surface Hub did sell well. While Microsoft never released sales figures, in the summer of 2016, I tried to buy two Surface Hubs to use in the background of my podcast, First Ring Daily, and every channel partner I called was out of the devices. If we wanted a single unit, we would have to wait 8 to 10 months.

Surface Hub 2X

Microsoft was incredibly proud of Surface Hub and the fact that it was being manufactured in the United States. Before all the delays and price changes, Microsoft let Fast Company tour its facilities in Wilsonville, Oregon to show how the devices were made in America. Each product was proudly stamped with Manufactured in Portland, OR, USA as Microsoft wanted the world to know it supported manufacturing jobs in the United States.

Two years after highlighting its factory, Microsoft quietly closed the plant and fired 124 employees along with dozens of contractors. The company was moving production of its next-generation device to China, ending the domestic production of Surface Hub.

Ultimately, Surface Hub was a success for the company but there were many lessons learned about manufacturing devices at this size, announcing hardware too early, and fully understanding the pricing models as well. But this wouldn't stop the company from building a second generation of the device that radically changed the agenda for Surface Hub.

For the second generation Surface Hub, Microsoft needed to simplify the production process: making two different sizes of the previous generation hardware created complexity and slowed down its output rate. The company went back to the drawing board and rather than simply updating the first generation device, it created something entirely new.

Surface Hub 2 is Stevie Bathiche's baby. He has been one of the primary driving forces behind this device and has put his soul into building the hardware. And on May 15, 2018, Microsoft showed off this next-generation device that the company said it planned to start shipping in 2019.

Hoping to avoid the mistakes of the past, Microsoft didn't announce a specific release date but instead gave a broad timeline for release. It also didn't reveal the price or final specifications. Despite its best efforts, however, Microsoft still managed to create confusion in the market.

At its Microsoft Ignite 2018 conference in September 2018, the company revealed that it was building not one model of the Surface Hub 2, but two. The first, called Surface Hub 2S, would run the same software as the original Surface Hub and would ship in 2019. The second, called Surface Hub 2X, would not ship until 2020, but it would run the new software that was originally promised.

As soon as this change in schedule was announced, speculation began that Microsoft had in effect delayed Surface Hub 2. After all, there was no mention of the two models or the extended schedule in the original announcement. And running the original Surface Hub software on Surface Hub 2 did not provide any of the improvements that were unique to Surface Hub 2, like the ability to rotate the display.

Once again, Microsoft had messed up a Surface Hub announcement and here's why that happened.

After Microsoft announced Surface Hub 2, the company received a significant amount of feedback from corporate customers that did not want to be running two different and incompatible iterations of Surface Hub. Microsoft listened to this feedback and started work on Surface Hub 2S.

Because Surface Hub 2 utilizes a modular compute unit, adding a second model didn't add a significant amount of complexity to the project. So even though Surface Hub 2S was not part of the original plans, the team was able to design the new model in about a month and then prepare to ship it in 2019.

Conveniently for Microsoft, this change also provided cover to extend the timeline for shipping what was now called Surface Hub 2X into 2020. Add in some marketing spin to make it sound like this was the plan from the onset of the project, and the company now extended the runway to releasing the product without it looking like a delay.

Delays aside, Surface Hub 2 embraces Microsoft's dream of a modular computer. The compute unit can be removed, it can be paired with other another Surface Hub 2 to expand the canvas, and it also has a unique rotating hinge that can be manipulated with one finger.

The same person who designed the Surface Dock in less than 24 hours also designed the rotating hinge for the Surface Hub 2. Microsoft refused to tell me this person's name as they keep it a closely guarded secret, and would only say that they work for Ralf Groene.

Following the announcement that Surface Hub 2X release would be pushed back to 2020, Microsoft decided to show off the device at Ignite 2018 to select members of the press behind closed doors. It wanted to emphasize that the product was real and not vaporware; this is important because the company had previously only shown off the hardware in a highly-polished announcement video. I was among those able to get a "hands-on" look at the device, but the company would not allow pictures or video.

Microsoft hopes that the Surface Hub's modular compute unit will make the device "future -proof," as the Surface Hub 2S can be upgraded to a Surface Hub 2X by swapping out this one user-serviceable part.

But as with everything Microsoft, it will all come down to the execution of the software and hardware teams to make the product live up to the experience shown off in the 2018 announcement video.

Chapter 24 - Let it Go

"We let someone else build it, a first for Surface"

Released in mid-2018, Surface Go is the spiritual successor to Surface 3. Both are tablet PCs that look like Surface Pro but in smaller, less expensive packages. And both launched in similar ways, without an in-person event. But for Surface Go, Microsoft purposely changed its naming scheme to avoid confusion with the Surface Pro line. And, of course, it couldn't use the Mini name. So the Go brand was born.

Surface Go is designed to occupy the bottom half of the Surface product family. Because the company never released a Surface 4, entry-level pricing for the Surface family had hovered at around $800 for the previous few years. Which means that if you were looking for a casual, inexpensive PC, the Surface brand wasn't for you.

Surface Go

Like many Surface products before it, Surface Go did leak: Bloomberg revealed that Microsoft would release a smaller Surface tablet in

May 2018. But the unique branding was kept a secret right up until the official announcement in July.

As was the case with Surface 3, Microsoft announced Surface Go with much less fanfare than it had with other Surface products.

Two weeks prior to the announcement, Microsoft invited some members of the press to New York City to get an early look at the device in small, isolated groups. It was a casual affair, held in private rooms above the Microsoft store in midtown Manhattan, with no stage, no live stream, and most importantly, no Panos Panay.

This was done intentionally. Microsoft uses its top executive to show the significance of events. If Satya Nadella shows up, it's a key moment for the entire company. And with Panay not personally announcing Surface Go, the company signaled that this product was less important than some of its other hardware bets.

But even though Panay was not there, Ralf Groene was. If accidentally.

While Paul Thurrott and I were being introduced to the hardware, Groene and his family walked into the briefing room. I'd like to think that he intentionally crashed the meeting because he knew Paul and I were there. But it was more than likely just a coincidence.

As always, Groene was his pleasant self and talked briefly about Surface Go before introducing us to his family. He explained how his daughter had helped design Surface Studio. And while the other Microsoft and PR teams in the room got a bit squeamish as Groene steered the conversation in a new direction as he usually does, he provided a unique perspective on the device that felt more genuine and less scripted marketing.

With its 10-inch 3:2 display, Surface Go was the smallest Surface device that Microsoft had ever sold; Surface Mini was smaller but had never made it to retail shelves. The big difference here was that this device was not using an Intel Atom chip: Microsoft used something a bit more powerful, and with a bit less stigma. Or so it thought.

Microsoft was very clear in the briefing that the Pentium Gold processor in Surface Go was not an Atom processor. The company reiterated this point many times, as it felt that the Atom branding had tarnished Surface 3. And it wanted everyone to know that this product was not following down that same path.

The Pentium Gold CPU helped keep costs down, but it wasn't exactly a high-water mark for performance. But what's odder is that Microsoft, prior to the release of Surface Go, had been championing a new Windows on ARM initiative based on Snapdragon chipsets created by Qualcomm, not Intel. For the company to release a small tablet that was not running on a Snapdragon chipset undermined its ability to confidently say that it believed Windows on ARM was a viable future for Windows.

As it turns out, Microsoft's decision to choose a Pentium Gold CPU was largely political. Intel had courted Microsoft heavily to use its chips in the device instead of Qualcomm's when it learned that Microsoft was leaning heavily in that direction during the design stages of development.

Because Microsoft was announcing the hardware virtually, the company took on a different set of challenges related to keeping the release a secret. With the press briefed about the hardware, everyone who saw the new product had to agree to an embargo which was set for 9 am ET on July 10.

With the embargo deadline rapidly approaching, Tom's Hardware accidentally published its Surface Go post early. When this happens, it sends the publications that had not broken the embargo into a frenzy. Should they push their content out immediately so as not to miss out on the traffic wave? Or should they wait for Microsoft to give clarification if plans would be changed?

Tom's Hardware was quick to retract its post and hide the content. But once something is posted to the web and it hits social media, there is no taking it back. The post was quickly cached by Google and the archives were quickly scooped up by publications not bound by Microsoft's embargo.

While embargo-breaking creates enough havoc for Microsoft, Surface Go's release was also the victim of the tech news cycle. On the day that Surface Go was released, August 2, 2018, Apple passed the $1 trillion market valuation. This was the same day that Surface Go reviews became available but Apple managed to steal a significant portion of the news cycle that Microsoft had hoped to capture.

Those who were watching this release closely may have heard several codenames for the product from various outlets. It was while digging up details on Surface Go that I learned that Microsoft typically utilizes two codenames for each product, one for marketing and the other for engineering, It does this in part to help shake out where leaks are coming from. But for this particular product, the company had three internal codenames floating around prior to release that all started with an L.

While every new hardware release has its risks, Surface Go was one of the safer bets for Microsoft. It already knew where and how to sell the product thanks to Surface 3, and Surface Go's lower price point meant that it should sell in higher volumes.

And by going with Intel and Windows 10 Home, not Windows 10 S, many of the marketing barriers of previous products were no longer an issue. The device was targeted at education and corporate clients for first-line workers; Microsoft sold 40,000 units to one customer before it was even released.

One final interesting note about Surface Go: This is the first Surface product that Microsoft released that was not fully designed and built in-house. Instead, Microsoft outsourced the engineering and production to Quanta Computers, which means it deviated from the previous generation Surface devices that were designed and built by the Surface team.

But, this is not entirely unusual in this industry. Apple has done this with its hardware and other PC makers have gone down similar paths.

Chapter 25 - Full
USB-Circle

"It was up to him, we already had to build something new"

Heading into the summer of 2018, Microsoft had a choice to make. Would it hold a hardware event in the fall as it had in the past, or should it simply refresh the hardware and use a soft release? While we now know that Microsoft did hold an event to announce some relatively minor product revisions, it wasn't a simple decision.

The company was a bit hesitant to host an event because it had made significant product announcements like those for Surface Book and Studio Studio in previous Octobers. Were it to host an event and only announce modest updates for its hardware, the response might be underwhelming.

And there was also this issue of "Andromeda." Microsoft's most loyal fanbase had been clamoring for this rumored foldable tablet/phone-like device for over a year and had been hoping to see it released in the fall of 2018.

Microsoft ultimately decided to host an event in New York City. But it also wanted to set the context for the press. On a brief but important call to let me know about its plans, Microsoft explicitly told me that there would not be any new form factors for the PC space announced at this event. The company made it clear that Andromeda was not going to happen.

Microsoft also kept this event much smaller than previous press events. About 65 people were invited to what was a more intimate environment for the smaller announcements. Additionally, the event was held at 4 pm, which was an unusual time. And because it was not a major Microsoft event, Satya Nadella was not in attendance.

In a somewhat awkward introduction, Microsoft used this time to talk a bit about Windows 10's newest release and to showcase an upcoming feature that would allow users to mirror Android apps from their phones to their PCs. While this part of the presentation itself was well-rehearsed, it also felt bolted-on to the hardware event and didn't fit within an overall theme.

Panay walked onto the stage after the Windows segment completed. And he wasted no time entering into his standard routine of explaining the importance of the products as well as talking about the future of the brand.

As he had done many times before, he left the stage and wandered around the room to engage the audience more personally. This type of thing had become a cornerstone of all of his presentations, and this time around, he nearly grabbed Mary Jo Foley's laptop until he realized it was an HP model. So he then grabbed Paul Thurrott's Surface Laptop instead. He held it up to talk about his products as he continued to walk around the audience.

At the event, the company announced a chipset refresh for Surface Laptop and Surface Pro, as well as a new black color that matched the original Surface Pro. It also announced an update to Surface Studio with a newer but still somewhat dated 7th-generation Intel chipset and 10XX series graphics cards.

I had been reporting on these new products for months, so these announcements were largely expected. But there was one update, or one non-update, that left many scratching their heads: Surface Laptop 2 and Surface Pro 6 both lacked a modern USB-C port, while the Surface Studio 2 included at least one such port.

This was confusing because Microsoft's entry-level tablet, Surface Go, had this port. As did Surface Book 2.

Microsoft had launched Surface Book 2 a year earlier, in November

2017 at an event that was by far their most relaxed to date. It more like a Q&A session than a staged presentation, though it had been held in New York City like most other recent Surface events. But this one was under embargo and there was no live stream. At a small venue in Manhattan, Panay wasted no time in unveiling the Surface Book 2, which came in both 13 and 15-inch models, both of which included a USB-C port as well.

With the company's two previous Surface releases including USB-C, it was puzzling that the newer Surface Laptop 2 and Surface Pro 6 did not. This was especially true because these are the two Surface products that had sold in the highest volume in the previous years.

And there was a reason: Panay didn't want it. This was not a technical limitation. Instead, Panay is said to have made the decision himself, so his engineers did not include the ports when refreshing the internals of the devices for the updated Intel chips.

Also, controversially, Microsoft had previously changed the naming scheme for Surface Pro so that the successor to the Surface Pro 4 was simply called Surface Pro and not Surface Pro 5. But when the company announced the sixth generation Surface Pro, it returned to naming it with a number and called it Surface Pro 6.

At the time of the Surface Pro (5), it was assumed that Microsoft was following Apple down the path of not including model numbers in its product names. But this idea was quickly reversed after it created a nightmare for support teams not knowing which version of Surface Pro a user was calling about.

Amidst all the minor updates announced in the fall of 2018, we did see Microsoft start to explore the boundaries of how far the Surface brand can be extended.

For years, the company had been using the Surface brand to only sell hardware and peripherals directly related to its primary PC business. There are Surface-branded smartpens, mice, keyboards, and docking stations, but in the fall of 2018, the company announced a pair of premium headphones. They were named Surface Headphones, of course.

Surface Headphones

These headphones weren't rebranded from another product. Instead, Microsoft began exploring how to build its own headphones three years earlier. And it wanted something that would beat the competition.

Product development took about 18 months. And with the company announcing the headphones alongside its refreshed Surface hardware; Surface Headphones became a primary focus for the event as it was the only truly new hardware.

Surface Headphones will be an interesting test of Surface brand loyalty. If the Headphones are successful, we can expect to see the Surface brand continue to spread horizontally to new types of hardware as Microsoft tries to build up a portfolio to rival Apple on every front.

But there was one oddity to the Surface Headphone announcement: Microsoft revealed the pricing ($349.99) but said that it would unveil the shipping date later in the year. As it turns out, it only waited a week to release that date.

So why didn't Microsoft simply announce the shipping date on stage at the event as it did with the rest of the hardware? As it turns out, the company has a policy, created in the wake of the Surface Book and Surface Pro 4 quality issues, by which shipping dates cannot be announced until the hardware reaches the so-called "Product Quality" milestone. And Surface Headphones had not reached that stage by the time the hardware event occurred.

But a few days after the event, the signoff happened. And Microsoft was able to finally announce a shipping date for Surface Headphones. Which, by the way, charges via a USB-C port.

Chapter 26 - The Past and Future

"You are never really done, the pipeline is always full"

When Microsoft started down its Surface journey, it was a big gamble to determine whether the company could not only build PCs but build some of the best PCs in the world. While we often hope that success comes easily, the truth is that it often takes time, hard work, and perseverance to make it happen.

The Surface brand is a classic story of the trials and tribulations of building a risky new business. But the rewards have far outweighed the risk. From a $900 million write-down to being the hero brand for the PC industry, Microsoft risked alienating its partners to chase down a future that it wanted to control. If Microsoft had abandoned Surface after Surface RT, the PC industry would likely look very different today.

But the road ahead is far from certain, the company will face new challenges going forward as it prepares to significantly update products like the Surface Pro, which is starting to show its age. The company has traditionally bucked the trend of releasing new hardware when Intel releases new chips, but it is also backed into a corner as it doesn't want to push out new hardware until it can also tout new performance gains.

Panay and his team continue to explore all options for an upcoming generation of new Surface products. But one thing holding them back, as of this writing, is Intel's ongoing struggle to release "Ice Lake," its more efficient 10nm chipset.

This setback impacts the release of a wide range of next-generation products. And it highlights Microsoft's dependence on Intel to power its hardware, and underscores its desire to also use ARM-based chipsets at the high-end too. But for the time being, it's (mostly) Intel going forward. And despite the sometimes tense relationship the two have had at times, they have a partnership that spans decades. That partnership won't change for the foreseeable future.

The question then becomes how Microsoft can continue to push forward with Surface.

In the second half of 2018, the company was recognized as being one of the top five largest PC vendors in the United States by unit sales. That's a major milestone, but it also means that there is plenty of headroom left for growth. That being said, Microsoft is not interested in competing for volume and will continue to focus on premium offerings; climbing much higher on the vendor list will be a significant challenge.

For the next generation, according to those familiar with the company's plans, Microsoft is exploring new opportunities with its hardware. An AMD-based Surface Laptop is a possibility, with a targeted release in the Q4 2019 timeframe. Microsoft is exploring using the AMD Picasso architecture but those plans may change as chips mature and performance and availability timelines become clearer.

For the company's flagship desktop, Surface Studio, bigger changes are on the horizon. While a refresh in 2019 is not currently in the cards, Microsoft will finally deliver a Surface monitor in the 2020 timeframe. But it will come with its own unique twist.

The modular compute design showcased first with Surface Hub 2 will make its way to Surface Studio. If one wants a standalone Surface display, this will likely be as close as you can get. That being said, the modular design, if it materializes as currently planned, will significantly change how we think about all-in-one PC designs and will allow for simple upgrades rather than having to buy an entirely new computer.

Microsoft's Andromeda device has evolved to be larger than most are likely expecting. While it was initially designed as a small form-factor product, the updated form factor is larger than that and is currently planned for a late 2019 release. This is an ambitious new design for Microsoft and is experimental in nature; the company does not need to ship this product, but it's a hardware device that the company believes could showcase the future of the PC.

The company first envisioned Andromeda as a pocketable piece of hardware with dual-screens and LTE connectivity. But after struggling to find a serious use case, and the fact that their previous mobile hardware had absorbed $10 billion dollars, the device went into the vault, for now.

Surface Book will also be updated, but that release may not come until as late as Q1 2020. The company is exploring new hinge designs for this product and the need for high-end performance parts may delay availability.

The company is also exploring a spring 2019 event as well, where it could show off a new type of Surface-branded ambient computing device. If that materializes, the product is designed to help deal with some of the common frustrations of using a smartphone. But I don't believe it is actually a smartphone.

And for the Xbox fans out there, Microsoft is exploring two revisions to the Xbox One S for 2019. One version does not have an optical disk drive and is designed to be the lowest possible entry price for the Xbox family. And the other will have a disk drive but will be cost-reduced when compared to the initial Xbox One S release.

Those who are concerned about having a large physical collection of games that won't work on a disc-less console will be happy to hear that Microsoft also plans to offer a disc-to-digital trade-in program. This program, exactly as the name suggests, will let you turn your physical games into a digital license and then download them on your new console.

And then there's the device that started it all, Surface Pro. This venerable product will get a significant refresh in Q4 2019. Expect to see USB-C, smaller bezels with rounded corners, and new color options as well.

These products are often a year or more from release at the time of this writing, so the plans could and will change. And many are heavily dependent on Intel's ability to bring its next-generation chips to market on-time. Regardless of any schedule changes, it is absolutely clear that Microsoft is charging forward with hardware and has no plans of slowing down.

And that future looks great for Microsoft. The company has finally found its stride in hardware, it has a much better understanding of the mechanics needed to produce premium hardware, and it has achieved its goal of setting a higher bar for PCs. While the company has yet to achieve the same level of admiration that is afforded to Apple, there is no doubt that Microsoft is headed down that path.

When Surface Studio was first announced, it was instantly compared to Apple's iMac. Surface Book was compared to Apple's MacBook Pro. And Surface Laptop was compared to Apple's MacBook Air. Even if Microsoft never achieves the same sales volume as its Cupertino cousins, one thing is for sure, it has successfully pushed back on the idea that Apple is the only company who can create innovative premium hardware.

For Microsoft, the Surface brand has become an invaluable asset. For a company that makes, and will continue to make, the majority of its revenue with software and services, Surface has been a rare bright spot in the consumer and hardware spaces.

During the past six or so years, I've had the opportunity to talk with Panos Panay, Ralf Groene, and Stevie Bathiche on and off the record. Each interaction with them is always light-hearted but also full of details about the challenge this team faces each day to bring hardware to the masses.

Any time you have a chance to talk with the people behind the

165

hardware, you understand that for them, this is more than a laptop or tablet. They know that this is their chance to make a lasting impression on the technology world and they will let nothing stop them from trying to push the envelope forward.

While writing this book, current and former Microsoft employees shared their stories about how this billion-dollar brand was born and the challenges they had to overcome. Their insights and information helped to add color to the stories that make Surface, Surface.

As an outsider who has been following Surface from the beginning, I will forever be grateful to those who have helped me along the way and hope that one day, I will be able to pay it forward.

CPSIA information can be obtained
at www.ICGtesting.com
Printed in the USA
LVHW042106121218
600231LV00002B/138/P

9 781790 395811